A Dangerous Wisdom

Gay Love Magic

Casey Giovinco

LIBRARY OF CONGRESS CATALOGUING-IN-PUBLICATION DATA

Includes bibliographical references.

Copyright © 2019 Casey Giovinco

All rights reserved. No part of this book may be reproduced or transmitted in any form or by any means, electronic or mechanical, including photocopying or recording, or by any information storage and retrieval system, without permission in writing from the publisher.

ISBN: 978-0-9998719-4-2

On the Cover: Artwork by Stewart A.
Project Editors: Thorn Nightwind; Stewart A.; and Shawn M. Shadow ("Afolabi"), Olorisha (Oni-Yemaya) and Spiritist (a.k.a. anxiety-ridden, nut-job, editor-in-chief).

ACKNOWLEDGEMENTS

Though the author usually gets all the credit, it is a rare author who actually does all the work of bringing a book to market. I am certainly not that rare author. This book could not have been written without the support and talents of many wonderful people.

First and foremost, I would like to thank Gala Witchcraft and, specifically, my coven in Greensboro, North Carolina for bearing with me during the writing process for this book. It beat me up tremendously. It touched on every insecurity and raw nerve I had, and there were times when I really wanted to throw in the towel. They were a constant source of strength and support for me in those dark times. Thank you.

I would also like to thank Shawn Shadow, Stewart A., Aaron Clevenger, and Thorn Nightwind for their help with reviewing and editing the book. Without their vigilance and commitment to my vision, A Dangerous Wisdom wouldn't be what it is today. Shawn not only supported me in my writing, he listened to me vent my frustrations and helped me to navigate the process to find solutions to problems which frustrated me immensely. Once again, Stewart's artistic vision served to inspire and help me understand the scope of this project and its impact on Gay men. Without Aaron triple checking my work, it would not have been as polished as it turned out to be. Thorn has always been a wealth of information for me and his kindness and generosity in sharing that information never ceases to amaze me.

Finally, I would like to thank Jack Register and Brad van Eeden-Moorefield for helping me to find legitimate psychological resources to back up my theories. I could not have done this without their research and insights.

Honestly, I am genuinely touched by all the support that I received toward making this book a reality. Thank you all.

CONTENTS

	A Note To The Reader	i
	Preface	ii
	Prologue	iv
	Introduction	viii
1	We Pretty Princes	1
2	Addicted To Love	18
3	What's Love Got To Do With It?	23
4	A Thoughtform Elemental Servitor	33
5	Self-Love … And I Don't Just Mean Masturbation!	42
6	Polarity & Gay Dating	55
7	Desire: Wanting It Bad Enough	64
8	How Magic Works: Intention & Belief	75
9	Mirror, Mirror	79
10	Sex & Regenerative Power	89
11	In Praise Of A Hookup	99
12	Gay Love	106
13	A Need-Fire Rite For Love	115

A NOTE TO THE READER

Dear Reader —

Your fairy godmother was deficient. She turned a pumpkin into a carriage, mice into horses, and a frog into a prince, but these are mere parlor tricks compared to the magic you and I will weave together. Besides, who needs to smell like a stale, ol' pumpkin when they're getting ready to go to a formal affair? Horses that cause black plague are just a dreadful idea on the face of it, and, as for a frog masquerading as a prince, where did she ever get that idea? F for effort, dearheart!

I might have been willing to forgive all that ham-handed *Bibbidi-Bobbidi-Boo* business if she hadn't also left you barefoot and broken-hearted, walking on broken glass, bloody and beaten and worse off than when she found you. It is because of that delusional ditz that you have unrealistic expectations of love and romance, and until we undo the damage that she has wrought, sorting out your love life will be extremely difficult. So, never being one for half-hearted measures … I arranged to have her hit by a bus!

Now, I'm taking over, and, unlike that Lisa Frank knock-off, I don't trade in fantasies. There will be no vegetable or animal transmutations here, no glass slippers nor misbegotten jabberwocky-style novelty songs. Instead, you will find tried-and-true occult wisdom, down-to-earth common sense, and sound magical practices that will empower you to achieve your own goals. That demented fairy may have strewn your hopes and dreams upon the floor, but don't worry. We're going to spin this mess of straw she left behind into pure gold!

PREFACE

Picture it. It's the 15th Century in Venice, and you are a young man born into one of the city's wealthiest families. You are secretly in love with a dark-haired beautiful gondolier named Lucio, and he loves you back. In fact, he loves you so much that he brings you into the *Old Religion*.

Though you have to keep your affair and your witchcraft hidden, it doesn't feel dirty to you. In fact, you know this is the most beautiful thing in the world, you know that your love for each other is transcendent, and both of you are uplifted by each moment you spend together.

Unfortunately, your love is revealed very publicly, and your Lucio is killed because of it. You are disowned by your family, and after losing everything, you die penniless, cursing your family with your dying breath.

You arrive in the Underworld with a vengeance, and you rail in your anger at the Horned God of Death and Resurrection. You swear that what happened to Lucio would never happen again.

The God, touched by your love and devotion to this man, shows you how you could heal this by reincarnating again, finding your way back onto the path of the wise, reuniting with your witches in life, and healing this hatred by living your life according to the old ways.

You agree, and are reborn with no knowledge of this mission, but somehow, you manage to find your way back to the witches who love you, back to your tribe, and together you heal. In healing yourselves, a ripple effect spreads out across time and space, and subtly begins to heal others, who eventually work toward finding their own place in this world.

It's a tale as old as time.

Something similar happened in ancient China in the Fujian Province. Hu Tianbao fell in love with a very beautiful imperial inspector. Though rank and decorum kept Hu Tianbao from declaring his love openly to this inspector, he couldn't help spying on the man through a hole in the bathroom wall. One day he got caught peering, and he confessed his love for this man, who had him beaten to death.

Upon reaching the Underworld, Death was so moved by Hu Tianbao's love that Death, himself, sought to right the injustice of the murder by appointing Hu Tianbao as the guardian of homosexual affections.

The knowledge that in death we will find the acceptance of the love, which we had hoped to find in life, is a theme in much of Gay Mythology. It's almost universal wherever there is rampant homophobia within the overarching culture.

As an author and the founder of Gala Witchcraft's initiatory line, however, I imagine a world where things like this, like what happened to Matthew Shepard, things like what happened to my dear friend Frankie (who was Gay-bashed last year), never happen again. I hope that this book will help you love yourself better. Hopefully, the love you give to yourself will ripple out, like vibrations through water, to heal those around you, and should you desire it, I hope this book will bring you a partner who will love you for who you are.

Blessed Be!

PROLOGUE

I think that Arthur Evans said it best in his book *Witchcraft and the Gay Counterculture*, so there's no reason for me to reinvent the wheel.

"This book is an attempt to record some of the things that professional historians usually leave out. It is one-sided, in that it is mostly concerned with the victims of Western civilization, rather than their rulers. It is subjective, in that it reflects my own personal value judgments and emotions. It is arbitrary, in that it picks and chooses among all the source material, accepting a few things here and there, but rejecting most as biased or unreliable."[1]

This is not just true of historical works. The same applies to occult material as well. Every metaphysical book is written from the perspective of the author. It bears the stamp of his bias and highlights the material that supports his agenda. Evans was just honest about his bias, and, being inspired by his integrity, I have decided to follow suit.

While I, personally, am accepting of everyone, this book is written for a very specific type of Gay man. First and foremost, this Gay man is either a witch, or at the very least, he is interested in witchcraft, Wicca, or another occult spirituality. Second, he wants to take his spirituality to the next level by incorporating real sacred sexuality into his magical practice. Too many people think that sacred sexuality is just an extension of their mundane fetishes. That simply isn't true.

Though this Gay man probably still has hookups (he may even hook up on a regular basis), he has started desiring a deeper connection from the men he has sex with; and his casual encounters have begun to leave him feeling unfulfilled. For the record, there is nothing wrong with still wanting a hookup. Let's face it, sometimes you just need to "take care of business." This book is not catering to the Gay man who is fulfilled by casual sex

---

[1] Evans, Arthur. *Witchcraft and the Gay Counterculture*. Fag Rag Books, 1978, p. 3.

and "No Strings Attached" encounters. Regardless of how this target Gay man chooses to have sex (whether casually, with one partner or several, whether he desires a monogamous, polyamorous, or an open situation), he has started wanting some measure of intimacy with these people and the current options available leave him wanting.

I make no apologies about my style of writing or the exclusive nature of the audience I'm speaking to. Most books are written for straight people, and Gay men have to translate the wisdom within their pages to fit into our lives. This book is proudly written for Gay men. If you, as a Straight, Bisexual, Transgender, Asexual, or Intersexed person, can translate its wisdom to fit into your life, great. There is actually a lot of material in this book that, if the reader took the time to translate it for him- or herself, would be extremely universal. If you fit into one of those other communities and you either can't find value in the material or you simply refuse to do the necessary translation to find value in it, that's okay too.

Furthermore, the few books actually written for Gay men only pander to our lust and give little else of value. If you want a book that glorifies the phallus or descends into orgiastic fantasy, this book may not be for you. I truly believe there is power in being a Gay man and that we, as Gay men, have every right to be proud of who we are and the role that our ancestors held for us. The historical, sociological, anthropological, and psychological evidence proves this fact, as I showed (albeit in a very cursory way) in *Garbed In Green*. It's time that we as Gay men, especially Gay male witches, reclaim that legacy. It's also time that the Gay Community grow up and stop acting like awestruck adolescent boys encountering their first dick.

Now, that we've addressed that, let's move on and talk about something of substance. We need to put sex into its proper place in our lives. That place should be one of balance, where sex is actually held sacred, a place where it can empower us and be a boon to our community instead of degrading us.

In an attempt to speak directly to Gay men, I have flouted the modern convention of using gender-neutral pronouns in my writing. Instead, I choose to write using traditional English grammar. For example, I do not refer to single, individual people as *they*. Though I am a big proponent of the fact that the word *witch* is a gender-neutral term, I refer to the individual witch using the masculine pronoun *he* in this book, just as I did in *Garbed In Green*. Attempting to pander to every possible contingent of the reading public only makes the text clunky and harder to read, and, because my target audience is exclusively Gay men, I have chosen to streamline the text and stick to masculine pronouns wherever I have the choice.

I mentioned Bisexuality above in my list of sexualities for whom I am not writing this book. Though that may seem dismissive, it is not meant to be so.

I am personally offended by the entire concept of Bi-erasure. (I acknowledge that it's a thing.) I also firmly believe that a huge portion of society is actually Bisexual to some degree, and I have a huge amount of respect for that form of sexual expression. I wish more people would be honest about their actual feelings regarding whom they love instead of just hiding behind safe and convenient labels that don't actually express who they really are, but that's a topic for another book. That said, I am not, personally, Bisexual. I have no experience with it, and I'm choosing not to speak about it beyond this prologue. However, standard Wicca is extremely accepting of Bisexuality, especially in women. There is no need for me to add anything to this book (or any other book on Gay Witchcraft) about Bisexuality. The material to help Bisexual men explore their magical paths with women already exists and is far better than anything I could write as an outsider. Read that material.

Unfortunately, the same cannot be said about helping the Bisexual man explore his love of men magically. So, to the extent that he wants to explore the homosexual side of his sexuality, this *Gay Witchcraft & The Male Mysteries* series of books can be a tremendous resource for him. If he is looking for information that includes the full scope of his sexuality and accounts for his love of women as well as men in the same book, this is not that book.

As for whether or not this book creates a definitive account of Gay history, I turn once again to Mr. Evans's elegant response: "There is no such thing as *the* authoritative Gay history, but as many Gay histories can exist as there are Gay visions. May they all be written."[2] This book, and the other books in this series, are just my own personal attempt to write one small piece of that history from my own perspective. To that end, I do my best to speak directly to the reader by using terms like *we* and *us* when referring to Gay men within the text. I also include my own personal experience with the topics being discussed so that you, the reader, can see that I have shared similar experiences and have actually used this material to heal my own damage surrounding sex, love, and relationships.

---

[2] Evans, Arthur. *Witchcraft and the Gay Counterculture.* Fag Rag Books, 1978, p. 3.

INTRODUCTION

No issue causes us more stress than love. Like a siren's song luring us in with the promise of bliss, we live in constant fear of the ever-present threat of self-ruin no matter how happy we are in the moment.

The instances of love ruining someone's life are so plentiful, I could write an entire book on that topic alone.

Of course, there is the standard drama. One of my favorites is listening to sad songs on repeat in the privacy of your room, like an emo teenager, until you've cried out your last gut-wrenching tear. Hardening your jaded heart against the affections and "inevitable rejections" of a future lover, or drowning your sorrows in liquor or something harder. Then there are the less common drama bombs like professional ruin, castration, and loss of life.

It's hard to believe now (especially with Melania Trump as First Lady), but there was a time where someone's past sexual indiscretions could end a political career. Andrew Jackson had the misfortune to fall in love with a married woman. They were wed in 1791, but her previous husband didn't officially file for divorce until 1793. According to historian Harriet Chappell Owsley, "The campaign which preceded this election was the most abusive and slanderous that his enemies could contrive and was unequaled in American history until the 20th century."[3]

In 1717, the British poet Alexander Pope commemorated a medieval story about Eloisa and Abelard. However, the real facts of their affair were more lurid than a modern-day soap opera. Eloisa was a wealthy young woman, and Abelard was her tutor and 20 years her senior. Naturally, they had a passionate love affair, but when her uncle found out about it, he castrated Abelard.

Any way you look at it, love is brutal for romantics, and let's

---

[3] https://www.smithsonianmag.com/history/rachel-jackson-was-original-monica-lewinsky-180963713/

face it, most Gay men are deeply romantic in one way or another, or, at least, we start out that way before the traumas of coming out into the Gay Community take root. Personally, I have seen this happen countless times in my own life.

In high school, I had the biggest crush on the captain of my wrestling team, who was two grades ahead of me. After he graduated, I started hearing rumors that he was bisexual. I practically developed an arrhythmia, my heart started to beat so fast!

For the rest of that semester, I had fantasies about what it would be like when he came back to visit before Winter Break. (We went to a small private school, and the recent graduates usually came back to visit their old friends.) Those fantasies were nothing like what actually happened, though.

Most teenage boys fantasized about sex. I didn't. I dreamt of intimacy and a deep, abiding connection that was so intense it couldn't be denied by either of us. I fantasized about my wrestling captain being so drawn to me that he couldn't imagine having eyes for anyone else but me. I imagined him falling head over heels in love with me, inviting me home to meet his family, taking me upstairs to his room to make out with me and cuddle. I dreamed of him getting down on one knee and proposing marriage to me after high school.

On the few occasions that I imagined us having sex, it was always passionate and more romantic than horny. We took our time, making love in the afternoon sunbeams, kissing, and spending long hours afterwards cuddling and drifting off to sleep. It was all so saccharine and totally unrealistic.

When Winter Break finally rolled around, he showed up on the last day of wrestling practice and asked if he could wrestle with me. I had practiced drills with him countless times before, but this time was different. His signature move was the scissor hold, and when he wrapped his legs around my waist and squeezed, I actually swooned. Feeling the air leave me, he wrapped his arms around me, and pulled me close against his body, and I could feel his heartbeat speed up. His breath on my neck drove me to distraction. I felt so exposed and so vulnerable, but I wouldn't have changed a thing.

After practice, we went to get dinner at Chili's, which was a mile from the school. I wanted to confess my feelings to him, but each time I tried, something pulled me up short and I quickly changed the topic, which only made him smirk.

After an hour or two, it became clear to me that he was just toying with me, like a cat with its prey. Clearly, he liked me too, but he was actually going to make me be the one to initiate the process.

I don't remember exactly how I stirred up the courage to do it, but I did finally manage to get the words out of my mouth, "Do you like guys?"

"I like you." There was that sly smile revealing the hidden freckle on the inside of his lip and the twinkle in his golden-brown eyes again. It made my heart skip a beat.

I guess he took pity on me, because he didn't make me say more. He grabbed my hand from across the table, and he asked if I wanted to get out of there, which I did.

We went to his car and made out in the parking lot for the better part of an hour. He guided my hands where he wanted them, and then after he was riled up, he asked if I would fuck him. I agreed, and he suggested that I get in my car and follow him back to the school parking lot. It was nearly 10 o'clock, and the parking lot would be dark enough to cloak our activities.

As I followed him, my body shook like I was shivering off the cold. I wasn't. In fact, I felt overheated, but I couldn't control my shaking.

When we parked behind the building, I went back to his passenger seat. We started kissing and touching each other again, and he quickly took off his shirt. His body always drove me wild, but that night was like the first time I was encountering it. I couldn't stop running my hands across his torso. His chest was rock hard, he had the most defined six pack I had ever seen, and his "happy trail" made my mind wander into wild and unchartered territories, which I wasn't used to exploring.

He ripped my shirt off over my head, and started to unzip my jeans, reaching inside them. It wasn't long before this heavy petting turned into full-blown intercourse, and, just like that, the moment he was done, it was over.

He let me get off, but it was rushed, and when we were both done, he made his excuses for why he had to call it a night. I can't say that I saw the signs. I didn't. I was the fool who called him the next day and the day after, and when he didn't respond, I began to leave a concerned message, asking for him to call me back, which he never did.

After about two weeks of trying to get his attention again, I finally conceded what had happened to me, but I didn't want to believe that he would discard me like that. I thought what we had was special. I convinced myself that he felt the same way for me that I felt for him and that there was no way he could deny his passion for me.

I was hurt and embarrassed. I felt used.

Eventually, I grew angry; but, instead of lashing out at him, I turned my anger inward. I called myself "stupid" for believing the hottest boy in school could ever love me back, and I retreated into myself.

It was a long time before I could let myself love again. Many men tried to love me in the meantime, but I never wanted to have sex with any of them. What happened that night in the car behind the high school broke me. He took something that I viewed to be sacred, the love between two men, and he made it base and dirty.

After that experience, I refused to have sex with anyone else that they didn't express their love for me before we got naked. I wanted traditional Victorian courtship or nothing. Let me tell you, that was a recipe for disaster. Guys fawned all over me in college, but as soon as they realized they weren't going to get laid, they turned their attentions to less "high maintenance" men. That only served to solidify my hatred of giving into sex with guys, and I turned an aversion into a rule.

In fact, when my lack of sexual desire became public knowledge in Boston's Gay Scene at the time, I got the nickname *Ice Queen*. Apparently, the joke was that if you tried to get too close to me your dick would get frostbite and fall off. I wore that name with pride.

I convinced myself that my ability to not be ruled by my sex drive was a strength that all these other Gay boys simply lacked. Not only did they lack it, they were weaker still for giving into their baser desires so readily and so often.

My distance and aloofness combined with my muscular body only served to encourage their advances further. Countless men tried to be the one to melt the Ice Queen's frozen heart. Each of them wanting to be able to claim the accolades of being special enough or clever enough to do what all the others had failed to do before them.

Despite my lack of desire for the act of sex itself, I still wanted other men to desire me. I wanted them to crave me so intensely that they couldn't help but become romantic, but that never happened. No one ever bought into my idea of romance. Most guys just gave up when they couldn't break through my icy exterior, and they moved on to more available lovers.

After a while, I turned my attentions to online dating. I went into a chatroom for Nashville, Tennessee, back when chatrooms were a thing. I really wanted a Southern husband. It's a weird fetish of mine, but I just love the accent. It does something to me.

After a few days of stalking the Nashville room, I met the most beautiful man I had ever seen until that time. He was 6' 3", lean and muscular with the most beautiful caramel colored tan skin. It made me jealous, because I'm downright reflective in my paleness. His hair was long and wavy and chocolate brown. The contrast it presented with his pale green eyes made him look otherworldly, like something out of an Anne Rice novel. When we finally moved to talking on the phone and I heard his voice for the first time, I was hooked.

Though it hurt me to develop the feelings I was experiencing for him, I convinced myself that long-distance dating was a better fit for me. It would allow me to get to know a guy mentally and emotionally without the physical getting in the way, which is what I've always wanted.

We talked every day, sometimes twice a day. After about a month of consistent phone calls, we agreed to meet, and, always being one for the grand gesture, I bought a plane ticket to go visit him in Nashville. To my surprise, the chemistry was as intense as it had been with my high school wrestling captain, but Josh also kicked it up a notch.

We spent five amazing days together. We made love, and it was amazing. It felt elevatory, even pure. It felt like our souls touched, not just our bodies, and he rocked my world in the way I had wished my high school wrestling captain would have done.

We shopped. We ate good food. We went out and danced. It

was perfect. He even serenaded me with Patti Labelle's song "The Right Kinda Lover," which made me tear up. To be honest, if I'm in a mood, it still does. His voice was amazing, and I was genuinely in awe. He told me that Patti actually brought him up on stage once when he went to see her in concert, and apparently, he blew the audience away, which I can believe. It's been nearly twenty years, and I am still wowed by that moment.

My flight back to Boston came all too soon, and we parted with tears in our eyes. I don't think I stopped crying until the plane landed on the tarmac at Logan Airport. In truth, I was a terrible mess. I must have looked like a drowned baby bird, because the entire flight crew made it their mission to cheer me up.

After that, I only saw him one more time. He came to visit me in Boston. Our entire relationship lasted exactly six months, but, like a fool, I fell in love with him and fell hard! After his trip up to visit me in Boston, he promised to call me over the weekend, but he never did.

A group of his friends had taken him to Atlanta for *Night In White*, and he avoided my phone calls the entire time. I was hurt, but I forgave it. I told myself, "he's just busy and having a good time." I told myself that, "he'll call when he gets back to Nashville on Monday," but the truth was I knew he wouldn't.

When I genuinely like someone and we're apart for a time, that person is still a priority for me. I don't get sidetracked or distracted or forget about them. In fact, I look forward to those brief moments of connection that we can wrangle together.

Thanks to my wrestling captain, this time I saw the writing on the wall, and I was pissed.

After seven days of being ignored, I saw him online and confronted him. Apparently, he met a couple at *Night In White*, they fucked, and he felt really dirty about it. His guilt got the better of him, and, according to him, he purposefully sabotaged our relationship. That was the last time I spoke to Josh.

He was über Christian and had an unholy amount of guilt around being Gay. His shame around sex made my own 1950s pearl-clutching attitude look downright lascivious. He also had been extremely damaged from a former fiancé who left him three weeks before their wedding to go back into the closet and date a woman. If he hadn't been so callous towards me, I would have had empathy for him, but even all these years later, I still applaud his former fiancé for dodging that particular bullet.

My heart had thawed only to break into a million little pieces once again. It took me six years to even look at another man after that. I couldn't risk the hurt and pain. The wound that I suffered from that experience cut me to the quick. I could not move on, no matter how hard I tried.

It felt like someone I loved had died. I grieved for the loss of that relationship as badly as I grieved when my father died, and I felt like a fool. How could I even compare the two events? My dad was a good man who genuinely loved me, and Josh couldn't even love himself. I felt like I was betraying my father's memory by continuing to compare the two losses in my mind. Fortunately, my mom is amazing. She told me that you have to let the heart feel. You can't judge it by reason's standards. A loss is a loss, regardless of whether or not it makes sense to you or anyone else.

That helped alleviate a great deal of my guilt, but every time that I attempted to go out on a date with someone else, I compared him to Josh, and the new guy would always come up lacking. He wasn't as pretty or as charming or as fun as Josh. Eventually, I just stopped dating.

Instead, I bought into the hookup culture. I met guys online or in a local cruising spot, but I never let myself feel for them. If they tried to get closer, I pushed them away. It wasn't until I found the coven where I was taught that my real healing actually began.

I embraced the idea that it didn't have to be an either-or proposition. It was very hard for me, but along that path of healing, I begrudgingly came to accept the fact that not everyone I had sex with had to become my future husband. Sometimes sex was just sex.

But, like many Gay men, the desire for something "more" never left. After realizing that my desire for this "something more" was unhealthy and reeked of desperation and insecurity, I had to re-evaluate.

Clearly the desire for a monogamous,[4] loving, romantic relationship was not going anywhere for me. It seemed to be part and parcel of my soul, but how could I transmute this desire for what many people would call a "soulmate"[5] into something healthy and realistic?

More to the point, this desire for "something more" whatever that means (whether in a monogamous relationship or not) seems to be a huge struggle that many Gay men share with me. What exactly is going on here? How can we fix it so that we find the love we want and stop hurting each other in the process?

That is what this book is all about.

---

[4] I don't want my reader to think that I am pushing an opinion here. There is nothing wrong with polyamory or any other consensual relationship between adults who love each other. I am merely stating my own preference and acknowledging the fact that though I have considered polyamory in the past, it just doesn't seem to be right for me at this time in my life.

[5] I don't like the term "soulmate." It creates a false sense of hope in a false construct. There is no such thing as only one love for any of us. In truth, any one of us can have countless meaningful loves in our lifetime. We can even have multiple meaningful loves at one time. The other reason that I don't like the term "soulmate" is because it implies that a piece of you is missing and that you need someone else to complete you. You don't!

1 WE PRETTY PRINCES

Once upon a time, there was a closeted Gay boy who lived in the country. He fantasized about journeying to the big city and living among other men who thought as he did. He imagined what it would be like to have sex with another man. He reveled in the bliss that their bodies brought each other, and he delighted in the intimacy which he felt they would share. He spent his days and nights dreaming about falling in love with this man, who he hadn't met yet, and declaring their feelings for the whole wide world to see. He even went so far as to plan out every detail of their wedding, and in his daydreams, he saw both families coming together in loving support of their union.

After high school he spent a few years working in his local town, saving up enough money for bus fare and a few months' worth of rent in the big city. That closeted Gay boy decided to "come out" to his family before leaving. They ridiculed him and threw him out on the streets. He took a bus to the Gayborhood[6] and rented the cheapest apartment he could afford as close to the action as he could get. During the day he worked at a local restaurant, and at night he worked at the "bookstore" (which, to his amusement and surprise, was really just a polite way to say "porn shop"). On his nights off, he would dance and drink at the Gay club.

As the months rolled by, our Gay boy began to become frustrated that he had yet to experience sex with another man. Talking to one of his co-workers at the restaurant, he found out

---

[6] I'm from Pennsylvania in the region between Philadelphia and Reading, so for me the Gay section of every major city is always called the Gayborhood.

that though he was "attractive enough," he was "Gay fat,"[7] and that apparently meant that the other Gay boys in the club wanted nothing to do with him. He was crushed. He quit his job at the porn shop. It really wasn't making him money anyway. He went to the local Gay gym and asked for a job there so that he could get his membership for free. Then whenever he wasn't working, he ran on the treadmill and lifted weights in the weight room. Day and night, any time he had free time, he hit the weights.

Pretty soon our little Gay boy had the body of a Greek God, and all the other Gay boys in the club wanted to sleep with him. He finally got to experience Gay sex, and though he liked it a lot, he eventually grew to want something with more substance. When that failed to happen, he began to feel the same sense of isolation he felt when he was "Gay fat," and he turned to his wise (albeit bitchy) waiter friend who told him, "Gay life is like a party train. People get on and party with you, but very few will travel to the final destination. Gay life isn't like straight society. Nobody wants to get married or settle down. So, just party and have fun while you can. Stop trying to be straight."

As hard as he tried to heed his friend's advice, he just couldn't make his heart stop wanting to find love, which eventually pushed other men away. They found him "needy" or "insecure." Pretty soon, he felt as alone in the middle of the Gayborhood as he did out in the country with his bigoted family.

Over the years, he did manage to date a few guys, but it always ended more abruptly than he wanted. Even when he was the one to end the relationship, he felt a sense of emotional whiplash from the speed at which things ended. Over several years of this recurring cycle, he turned inwards again, became jaded and bitter, and went back into a protective space very similar to the closet of his youth.

This is not entirely my story. Elements of it are, but in a way, if you're reading this, elements of that story probably belong to

---

[7] The Urban Dictionary defines Gay fat as "A gay man who does not have a gym-perfect body, but rather carries a body fat percentage in the 12% - 20% range. A man who is considered gay fat within the community would likely be considered athletic, physically fit and in-shape within the greater cultural context."

you as well. Maybe you are isolated out in the country. Maybe you were abandoned by your family. Maybe you have been called "Gay fat," (which, for the record, is the stupidest thing I've ever heard in all my life. Go back and bitch-slap the son of a bitch who called you that. Okay! Okay! Maybe don't bitch-slap him. Just make a poppet of him and stuff it with lard. That'll teach the shallow bastard!). Maybe you identified with the guy who wanted a relationship but couldn't get anyone else to cotton on. Perhaps you are struggling with issues of aging, or you're getting jaded and bitter because your heart has been hurt for too long.

I empathize. Though I did move from the suburbs to the big city for college, my family has always been incredibly supportive of everything I do. My mom even bought and, to my horror, read *Garbed In Green*. She's just that awesome! I did dream of the big city and of finding other Gay men to be my friends, which many of them were not interested in doing. One Gay man even told me that he had enough friends. If I wasn't willing to fuck, he had no need to have me in his life. During a shopping trip for a bathing suit to wear to the beach, an ex-boyfriend-turned-friend did call me "Gay fat." He only did that once, for the record. (No, I didn't make the lard poppet of him. Though I thought about it.) I did plan my wedding out in every finite detail, except for the identity of my actual husband, and an older Gay man, who was a family friend, did actually tell me that bit about Gay life being like a party train.

It might also help to have some context here. This older Gay family friend had lived through the '70s and the AIDs crisis. During that same visit to his house in Manayunk,[8] he showed me his old photo albums from those eras. Whenever my eye would be drawn to a particular man, he would say, "Oh! He died." It was very matter-of-fact, and, after I got through that first album, I could see why. Literally, every single person in those albums, other than him, had died of HIV or some other HIV-related

---

[8] Manayunk is a part of Philadelphia. It has a small-town vibe, with row houses, lofts and Victorian homes occupied by young families and long-time residents. Along its hilly streets, the steep incline of "The Manayunk Wall" punishes riders in an annual bike race. Galleries and boutiques line Main Street, while its trendy eateries and boisterous bars evoke the area's Lenape name, "the place to drink."

complication.

His experience and his advice, jaded and misbegotten as it was, was a product of his era and the fact that he had aged out of his community. Everyone who would have been his age was dead, and the young boys no longer wanted him. Truth be told, he wouldn't have wanted to have sex with anyone his age had they even been around. He said so himself during that fateful visit not long before he took his own life.

The truth is that being a Gay man is downright brutal, but it is especially brutal for a romantic Gay man in today's app-obsessed hookup-culture-dominated Gay Community. If you are one of those romantic Gay men I'm speaking to, don't stress. You are not alone. Your situation isn't hopeless, and you don't have to let your frustration over being lonely embitter your soul or jade your broken heart. Remember what I said in the letter to the reader at the beginning of this book. I am going to be your fairy godmother, and we will work through this together. The romanticism that we both suffer is the very straw that we are going to spin into gold.

However, like Rumpelstiltskin's magical feat in the fairy tale, our own magic in this case will be a clever bit of transmutation. Actual romance is not the problem, but romanticism is. Romance is defined as a feeling of excitement and mystery associated with love. There is nothing wrong with that. In fact, most people would argue the excitement and mystery are essential to happy long-term unions. That said, romanticism is a different beast entirely. Romanticism is actually defined as "a movement in the arts and literature that originated in the late 18th century, emphasizing inspiration, subjectivity, and the primacy of the individual." This is the period that most of our commonly-known fairy tales were written in. Notice the "primacy of the individual" bit in that definition, though. Romanticism emphasizes the individual as a part of its thoughtform,[9] which means being obsessed with romanticism will actually keep you single.

In my tradition, which descends from one of the covens in Sybil Leek's Horsa Tradition, we talk about Sybil's eight tenets all

---

[9] For a better understanding of thoughtforms in magic, the reader couldn't do any better, in this author's opinion, than to turn to the Theosophists for clarification.

the time. They are beautiful and incredibly useful in helping a witch properly order his life. While reviewing Sybil's Tenet of Humility the other day, it dawned on me that romance, real romance, is actually an outcropping of humility.

Humility, as witches understand it, is an acceptance of the nature of things as they are. It has nothing to do with degrading oneself or the false modesty of the Christians. Instead, it teaches us that the past is necessarily the past and can't be changed. It asks us to be okay with that. This tenet encourages us to live in the moment and accept nature's course in the present circumstances; and, with regard to the future, it instructs us to not worry needlessly about things that haven't happened yet.

Something really wonderful happens when you apply the Tenet of Humility to romance. Being in the present moment will bond you and your partner closer together. Experiencing the joy and bliss that comes from indulging in the excitement and mystery of your love for each other, and finding happiness in the mundane aspects of your life together are what real romance is about. This is why we must transmute the base metal of romanticism into the pure gold of actual romance.

While writing this book, I went through my own alchemical journey on this exact topic. I confronted my desire for Prince Charming to ride up on his white steed and save me. I acknowledged that I had unrealistic expectations of other men and that I needed to find a different way to approach dating. I tried the hookup apps, thinking I was being unduly harsh about them, and, ultimately, confirmed that I wasn't wrong.[10] Hookup apps bring out the worst aspects of Gay men. So, I deleted all of them.

Step by step on this journey, I experimented on myself. I questioned everything. When I lacked the intellectual or emotional resources, I turned to the witches in my tradition. I went to the library and researched. Then I applied what I learned. I took a relationship coaching class as part of my continuing educational units for my philosophical consulting practice. I made YouTube

---

[10] Despite the fact that it appears like there is nowhere else to meet men, hookup apps really are not useful in helping Gay men find love. Granted some people have found their partners on these apps, but they are the exception, not the rule.

videos of my homework assignments. Through these actions, I had accountability toward reaching my goal of healing my sexual and emotional dysfunction. (Thank you all for your help in that, by the way.)

I did everything possible, because I knew that I had to either heal this part of myself or be alone forever. Even worse than that idea though was the idea that you, dear reader, were silently suffering the same fate someplace far away with no one to comfort you. I have my witches and my magic. Technically, I could cast a love spell and find a partner any time I wanted, but what do you have? When asked if being skyclad was essential to witchcraft, Sybil Leek jokingly said that she could cast a love spell wearing six fur coats. Descending from Sybil Leek, I know my magic works, but I didn't cast that love spell. I didn't cast it because, knowing how magic works, I didn't want to repeat the obscenely dramatic cycles of my past.

Magic doesn't just follow one's intention. It follows one's belief; and for the longest time, I could not believe that I would find someone worthy of being in love with in the Gay Community. Part of the reason for that was because, like many of you, I bought into the idea that the apps, the bars, and the clubs were the only places that Gay men had available to meet each other. So, when I looked at the apps, I was severely disappointed in what the Gay Community had to offer. I genuinely wanted no part of it.

The truth is that the apps are not the whole of the Gay Community, neither are the bars nor the clubs. I know it's tough to accept, because all the evidence in your experience points to the contrary. As witches, however, we are in a much better position to evaluate and address this topic than the vast majority of Gay men. We are part of an occult religion that revels in hiding wisdom in plain sight. Just because the rest of society told us that magic didn't exist, didn't mean we stopped searching for it. They used science, dogma, fear, and ridicule to throw us off our course, and we pushed through all of that to find our truth and our bliss. We are a strong and determined lot, we witches. If we can persevere in our search for magic, we can certainly accomplish the same feat with our desire to find a healthy version of the Gay Community and the love we desire so badly.

The first step to healing this particular damage, though, is understanding the root cause of the romanticism we find ourselves bathed in. The truth is we have been indoctrinated into this point-of-view. We didn't make it up out of whole cloth. As my mom always says, we didn't "lick it off the wall." Disney, Hallmark, the fairy tales our parents read us as children—these all laid the foundation for our current discontent.

It all started with the image of a silent, submissive, powerless, and beautiful young thing who was in an untenable situation, the kind of situation we wouldn't wish on our worst enemy. The suffering was great, mythic even; but, predictably, it was born with grace and good humor even though there was no possible hope of relief. Suddenly, a magical being (usually a fairy godmother, an animal, a witch, or a ghostly ancestor) stepped in to change this dreadful fate. Through one predictably romantic event after another, we witnessed the unfolding of a star-crossed love that overcame all obstacles and culminates in a wedding that would make the House of Windsor green with envy.

It always ends with the wedding. Beyond that, nothing is said. They live happily ever after, and we're left with the nagging question: How?!

We all know this story. There are countless versions. In fiction, the girl can be poor and downtrodden. In real life, she rarely is. In both cases, the role is always filled by a woman in our modern imagination.

Grace Kelly, Jackie Onassis, Diana Spencer—none of these real-life Cinderella's were ever poor or downtrodden in any real sense. The mere fact that each was chosen by their respective princes and elevated to the heights of glory through his love still worked to perpetuate the romantic idea that we can all achieve a comparable level of glamour and acceptance from wedding our own chosen princes.

As damaging and problematic as this story is for straight women, the narrative is a bit more masochistic when it comes to Gay men. The glass slipper clearly does not fit us at all, but rather than find more comfortable footwear, we cram our toes into a shoe five sizes too small, risking breaking the glass and cutting ourselves to ribbons in the process. If it works at all, the true love fairy tale only works in a heteronormative construct where the man is willing to be the supporting character who propels the princess's story ... or, at least, that's how it looks on the surface. However, because we have no stories of our own, no models to emulate, Gay men desperately try to fit the proverbial square peg into the gaping round hole that exists in the very middle of this fairy tale structure.

Though he most certainly exists, it is a rare Gay man who fantasizes about being the prince to bring status or acceptance to his partner by rescuing him out of his life of drudgery and despair. That supporting role seems reserved almost exclusively for straight men who don't mind being relegated to the rank and file of "happy wife, happy life" drones.

Gay men, however, want to be the star of the show or nothing at all. No Ethel Mertz for us. We'll either be Lucy or you can cancel the cable bill. I'm guilty of this myself, for the record. I genuinely would rather make my own way unencumbered by a disappointing lover than have to be the prince in someone else's story.

It's understandable why few, if any, Gay men would relish being compared to Onassis or Prince Charles. As Gay men, we do appreciate a certain amount of beauty and aesthetic style, but neither Onassis nor Prince Charles had any style or beauty to speak of. However, our resentment over being compared to Prince Rainier is a bit astounding. Yet, we do resent when our partners want us to fulfill the role of the prince. This is true, even when our version might look more like the debonair Prince Rainier than either of the other two suitors mentioned. Instead, we fight viscously to be cast as the Gay male equivalent of Cinderella, Snow White, or any of the countless other damsels in distress (whatever that might actually look like for two men in a romantic relationship, because we genuinely don't know).

In addition to wanting all the false privilege, which we wrongfully ascribe to the role of being cherished and adored like the Disney-styled fairy tale princess, Gay men also have the unhealthiest sense of entitlement that comes with being raised to be little princes from birth. What's more, we're not quite ready to give up our royal privilege to fill Cinderella's shoes. In my opinion, this is the central issue of our dating dilemma.

This desire to have our cake and eat it too really does a number on Gay men's social, sexual, and romantic interactions with each other. The only way the Cinderella role works, and whether it works at all is debatable, is if Cinderella is grateful, submissive, and truly powerless. One cannot be both the Prince and Cinderella in the same moment. We all want the privileges of both roles (Cinderella's glamour and the adoration bestowed upon her AND the Prince's right to choose and be respected); and, we feel entitled to both sets of benefits without having to suffer either role's disadvantages.

Vera Sonja Maass says it best when she says, that the prince "does not expect [his chosen partner] to look critically at him and his personality traits and offerings. That he approaches ... as a prince is sufficient evidence for his value, and he expects blind commitment ...".[11] To see the truth behind Maass's statement, all one has to do is look to apps like Grindr and Scruff. They are filled with Little Lord Fauntleroys whining about what they will and won't accept, trying to take everything they can from their haphazard interactions with each other and give back nothing in return.

We play the most unfortunate power games with each other on those apps. Some guys refuse to show their face so that they can't be tagged as Gay. Others demand to see face pics because they refuse to interact with someone ugly. Some, lack respect for the insecurities that other guys have about being labeled as Gay, and the potential public shaming that happens when one does come out of the closet. Some people refuse to send any pictures at all until the other guy has sent his first, and some merely ask for pictures and then ghost the person they were talking to. Some people refuse to chat without seeing X-rated pics, and others make demands about not seeing them. Still more have very strict physical, intellectual, racial, or socio-political requirements about what they will and will not tolerate listed on their profiles before you are even given a chance to talk with them.

Over and over again in our interactions with each other on these apps, we play the most pathetic political games in order to

---

[11] Maass, Vera Sonja. *The Cinderella Test: Would You Really Want The Shoe To Fit?*. ABC-CLIO, LLC: 2009, p. 15.

prevent our fear of the other guy abusing us. It really is a vain attempt to determine which prince's court we are operating in. We demand that they pay tribute to us (like we were actually princes in more than just our imaginations. Whether we admit to this consciously or not, we act as if we refuse to acknowledge these men as our equals (or even as real people) who exist beyond the tiny squares on a cell phone screen. We all have a "my way or the highway" attitude towards each other on these apps, and nobody seems willing to give each other the benefit of the doubt.

As muddied as the role of Cinderella is for Gay men, for women the role is crystal clear. It's all about gilding their cages. By teaching that validation and success come with the prince's approval, fairy tales are subliminally teaching young girls that they cannot find any measure of success without the prince's (a man's) support. The fact that fairy tales make the role of adored princess look so appealing, the fact that they provide her subservient role with some small measure of glamour is part of the trap. Give women just enough comfort and make them the envy of every other woman in the process and they won't even want to fight you. They'll maintain the trap themselves and mistakenly believe they're getting what they actually want.

Cinderella is nothing more than the prince's crown jewel. She's not a person. She's not even the main character in her own story. The Prince is. Outside of the fairy godmother, the Prince is the only person with agency in the entire story, the only one who has any real power to speak of. Now, you may be tempted to say that the evil stepmother has power, but she's as caught up in the hunt for a husband as any other woman. She knows her power is granted by men. She just refuses to delude herself of that fact, which is a far cry from being truly powerful on one's own.

However, because of the glamour and beauty associated with our favorite damsel in distress, real women fight to be just like her, and, unfortunately, so do Gay men. We all vie to give up our status as free agents in favor of being some man's "partner," which is really to say his trophy.

It has been argued that the Cinderella story is the best-known fairy tale in the world. If that's true, that would certainly account for its hold over our collective imagination. However, whether that's true or not, versions of it can be found in every country on earth. "Some scholars believe the folktale originated in the Orient, but it is impossible to prove that fact; all that can really be said with confidence is that the earliest known text [of this story] dates from the ninth century in China."[12] With about an equal amount of confidence, I can say that it is a crying shame that the Disney-version is all that most of us really know.

The Disney version is, in and of itself, a perversion of an earlier 1697 French version of the same tale. The essential incidents of the story, as Disney and his French predecessor, Charles Perrault, detail them are an ill-treated heroine, the midnight curfew, and recognition by means of a glass slipper. However, the pre-Perrault versions have so much more to offer us. It is in these older versions that we can see the power that Cinderella once claimed for herself. She wasn't merely some passive bauble glorifying a prince with her beauty. She was a force to be reckoned with, a power within her own right.

As a story about how to effectively navigate sibling relationships, Cinderella (or any of the variations on the theme) could be extremely useful in helping parents create harmonious relationships between their warring children. Bruno Bettelheim tells us that "'Cinderella,' as we know it, is experienced as a story about the agonies and hopes which form the essential content of sibling rivalry; and about the degraded heroine winning out over her siblings who abused her. Long before Perrault gave 'Cinderella' the form in which it is now widely known, 'having to live among the ashes' was a symbol of being debased in comparison to one's siblings, irrespective of sex."[13] Bettelheim goes on to talk of Ashenputtel, a German folk tale in which the male hero faces similar troubles with his own brothers. However, the male version of Cinderella doesn't stop with Ashenputtel. Bettelheim says, "There are many examples in the German language of how being forced to dwell among the ashes was a symbol not just of degradation, but also of sibling rivalry, and of

---

[12] Brown, Mary Ellen, and Bruce A. Rosenbery, editors. *Encyclopedia of Folklore and Literature*. ABC-CLIO, LLC: Santa Barbara, California, 2009, p. 130.

[13] Bettelheim, Bruno. *The Uses of Enchantment: The Meaning and Importance of Fairy Tales*. Alfred A. Knopf Publishing: New York, 1976, p.236.

the sibling who finally surpasses the brother or brothers who have debased him. Martin Luther in his Table Talks speaks about Cain as the God-forsaken evildoer who is powerful, while pious Abel is forced to be his ash-brother (Aschebrüdel), a mere nothing, subject to Cain; in one of Luther's sermons he says that Esau was forced into the role of Jacob's ash-brother. Cain and Abel, Jacob and Esau are Biblical examples of one brother being suppressed or destroyed by the other."[14]

In one analysis of one of the many versions of this tale, Cinderella is a shamanic story about passing the power through matrilineal lines. It holds hidden secrets of the art and provides instructions on working with ancestral spirits. Invariably, the magical being in these versions is the girl's deceased mother, passing on knowledge and guidance from beyond the grave. In another shamanic analysis of other versions of this tale, Cinderella's relationship with the various magical animals speaks to her otherworldly powers. However, in my personal opinion, the most interesting analysis of Cinderella for witches paints her as an incarnation of the Greek Goddess Hestia. Having a goddess as the source of this particular story would also explain its vast universal impact.

It goes a bit like this: "That Cinderella is the guardian of the hearth is well-proven. But she is not invariably the youngest child, especially when she is a stepchild. Mr. Gomme has pointed out that the Greek Hestia was the eldest child of Kronos and Rhea, and the goddess of the household sanctuary, or rather the fire burning on the hearth. Among the Ovahereró tribe of South Africa 'the eldest unmarried daughter of the chief has charge of the sacred fire, since this must never be allowed to go out.'"[15]

In the older, pre-Perrault versions, Cinderella might actually serve as a role model to empower women (and possibly Gay men), especially magically-inclined women and Gay men, but the modern versions of this story that we are all so familiar with

---

[14] Bettelheim, Bruno. *The Uses of Enchantment: The Meaning and Importance of Fairy Tales.* Alfred A. Knopf Publishing: New York, 1976, p.237.

[15] Cox, Marian Roalfe. *Cinderella Three Hundred and Forty-five Variants.* Publications of the Folk-Lore Society: London, 1893, p. xxxvi.

certainly aren't doing that. Instead, the modern versions teach insecurity and a lack-mentality. They feed our discontent with the drudgery of the daily grind and promise us pipe dreams that harm us more than they help. More to the point, they leave so many people out of the equation. Told from the heteronormative perspective, they isolate straight women from the rest of the world, and they leave Transgender people, Lesbians, and Gay men out of the story altogether.

One of the very real problems with Gay male dating post-Cinderella is that, like the ugly step sisters, we find ourselves barefoot before the possible future partner. Neither shoe truly fits us. We can't put on the hallmark glass slipper and be elevated to the status of adored princess and we can't bend the knee to another regal man without diminishing our own status as prince in the process. So what are we, Gay men, to do?

My first suggestion is to embrace the idea that the Gay Community can be so much more than the hookup apps, the bars, and the clubs. Whatever you have to do to make that real for yourself, begin that process immediately. Join a Gay softball league. Join the local Gay men's chorus. Make friends with other Gay men online instead of turning every interaction into a search for a future partner. Talk about shared interests, like Witchcraft or the occult.

My second suggestion (and, admittedly, this may be too difficult for some of you) is to give up the apps and all other incarnations of hookup culture. That does not mean that you can't have sex outside of a relationship. People have emotional and physical needs that must be taken into consideration, and that includes sex. Being in or out of a relationship doesn't change that fact. How we go about getting those needs met is the crux of the issue. If you are looking to find a loving, committed relationship that is more than just a hookup or a casual sexual experience, give up the reliance on hookup culture.

Finally, and I cannot stress this enough, you must kill Prince Charming. For the record, you're also going to have to release any connections between yourself and Cinderella … and all the other would-be princesses in your romantic imagination. The bottom line is that these two archetypes cause more damage than they do good. If you really want to be happy with another man, you must accept that you are not an archetype but a real person who is more complex, more beautiful, and more flawed than that; and, you'll have to accept the same things about your partner. If you are one of those romantic Gay men, like me, and you are finally ready to commit to your journey of finding a lover who will actually enrich your life, then it is time to kill off Prince Charming. He's preventing you from finding happiness with a real man, and, worse, he's hurting you. If you decide to go forward with this magical act of regicide, you will want to begin constructing an effigy of Prince Charming immediately. Take the idea of a scarecrow, and embellish upon this concept in your own creative way. Use a dried gourd as his head. Make sure that the gourd will be able to hold liquid during the ritual, so don't cut any unnecessary holes in it.

Find pictures that represent Prince Charming to you. Take pages from fairy tales. Get creative, but stuff your Prince Charming effigy with as many symbols of his role in your life as possible.

Finally, after some intense soul-searching where you take stock of your love life, accounting for your successes, and cataloguing the places where you failed to achieve your desired result, write a petition to get you back on track, something that eliminates Prince Charming's hold on you. Don't be flowery or grand in your language. Keep it simple. As I said in *Garbed In Green*, "Use clear, concise, simple, modern language to craft the intention. Like your affirmations, write the petition in positive language in the present tense."[16] For me, I might write something like: "I find real romance in every situation" or "I accept my lover for who he actually is." If it wasn't fantastical or earth-shattering, it wasn't romantic to me. The truth is that real romance is appreciating the mundane, day-to-day moments of joy with each other. There's nothing Disney about it. My petition might need to remind me of that. Alternatively, I also struggled to accept flaws in past partners, and this hurt quite a few of the men I dated. Today, I regret that. I might just as well write a petition to that part of my damage and,

---

[16] Giovinco, Casey. *Garbed In Green: Gay Witchcraft and the Male Mysteries*. Publisher: Casey Giovinco, 2018, p. 106.

in doing so, avoid hurting anyone else in the future. Whatever you decide to write, place your petition inside the effigy before the ritual. Make sure everything you stuff inside him will burn, though, because you are going to reduce him to ash!

In *Garbed In Green*, I talked about the historical practice of head hunting and claiming an enemy's power for oneself by "cleaning out the skull, gilding it, and using it as a sacred drinking cup in various rituals."[17] Obviously, it would be grossly inappropriate to actually decapitate someone and use his head as a drinking cup. I'm not advocating that you do that here. Modern witches do try our best to obey the law of the land. Fortunately, these ancient head-hunting practices evolved over the centuries. In *Garbed In Green* I also say, "As society evolved along 'civilized' channels, the significance of drinking from a skull was transferred to a ritual cup."[18] To fulfill the spirit of this ancient practice without breaking any laws or unnecessarily transgressing any current societal taboos, I highly recommend you find yourself a gourd to use as Prince Charming's head and sacred cup.

Give yourself two weeks to a month to prepare for this ritual. You may need that time to find and construct the supplies for this rite. You may also just need that long to search your soul to fully prepare for the working you're about to do.

Consecration of the Gourd

On a night of Venus (for Prince Charming's power is certainly Venusian) when the Moon is either Waxing or Full, pass the dried gourd through an incense of ambergris or musk and think of claiming Prince Charming's seductive power for yourself. Also think about the ancient head-hunting rites and visualize the gourd as being Prince Charming's skull. Then place the vervain, violets, and thyme inside the gourd one by one. and say:

"With these herbs, I sanctify this vessel to the

---

[17] Giovinco, Casey. *Garbed In Green: Gay Witchcraft and the Male Mysteries.* Publisher: Casey Giovinco, 2018, p. 55.

[18] Giovinco, Casey. *Garbed In Green: Gay Witchcraft and the Male Mysteries.* Publisher: Casey Giovinco, 2018, p. 55.

gods of love. Vervain is his power to invoke love in others. Violets are his power to generate lust. Thyme, his courageous and energetic mien."

Pour the spring water over the herbs and say:

"Blessed be the Sweet Water from which these seductive gifts first came. May the Sweet Water carry his power to me."

Leave the gourd outside in the light of the Full Moon, making sure to retrieve it before sunrise. Wrap it in a clean silk cloth and store it away in a safe place until the night of the ritual. Now this vessel will serve as the source of Prince Charming's Power for you.

During the preparations for the next phase of this ritual, journal about your past dating experiences and uncover any places where Prince Charming has had an influence on your behavior. Analyze those experiences. How did they influence you? What would have been different if you had abandoned your desire for an ideal mate and met the men in your past where they were at in the moment? What would it have been like if you had embraced your own interpretation of love instead of borrowing the fairy tale variety?

Look at everything. Re-read fairy tales if you have to. Uncover every place that this archetype has had an influence on you. Don't be fooled into thinking that Prince Charming is just some Disney hack. He comes in all shapes and sizes. Do you like the Tom of Finland men? That's Prince Charming. Do you prefer the typical depiction of a pretty, smooth, muscular Gay boy? That's Prince Charming. Do you prefer the archetypal bear or otter imagery? Those are also Prince Charming. Daddies? You guessed it. That's definitely Prince Charming.

Prince Charming is a clever bastard. He uses our ideals against us. It doesn't matter what the ideal. He can become it. For one man, he's the typical image given to us by fairy tale—a wealthy, beautiful, sexually desirable man who sweeps in and rescues us from our life of drudgery. For another, he is a sexual fetish. For someone else, he is a sense of community (like bears, cubs, and otters). Don't be fooled into thinking he is just one type and that you are immune to it. He is the ideal lover—whatever that is to you.

If you're not dealing with someone on authentic terms, if you're holding yourself or them to an unrealistic standard, if you're disappointed by the mundane nature of your interactions or you're just looking to infuse your life with some excitement by using someone else to do it, you're buying into a Prince Charming situation. Root him out! Journal, and build the effigy as you secure or create your tools for this rite.

The Sacred Claiming

On a solar night when that planet's power is strongest and the Moon is Full, build a pyre in a secret place. Take with you the effigy of Prince Charming with his consecrated dried gourd head. An anointing oil made of Frankincense essential oil in a base of jojoba, which should be made ahead of time. Bring along plenty of fresh ground frankincense to toss on the fire as an incense throughout the ritual. You will also want to bring with you any tools necessary for the making of holy water. Some witches will use a combination of salt or hyssop and spring water. You may want to have an athame on hand to empower the mixture. If you have your own method of making holy water, feel free to improvise here. Last but not least, don't forget the drumming music and the wine.

(1) Anoint yourself with the Frankincense oil, then carry the holy water around, asperging the Circle area moving widdershins from the North of the pyre back to the North. As you do, say:

> "May all my cares and sorrows be washed clean."

Place the holy water back by the pyre and light the fire.

(2) Dance widdershins around the pyre to raise energy for your working as the flames begin to leap along with you.

(3) Invoke the God.

> "Father of ages, guide of prosp'rous deeds,

The world's commander, borne by lucid steeds.
Immortal Fire, flute-playing, bearing light,
Source of existence, pure and fiery bright;
Bearer of fruit, almighty lord of years,
Agile and warm, whom ev'ry power reveres.
Bright eye, that round the world incessant flies,
Doom'd with fair fulgid rays to set and rise;
Dispensing justice, lover of the stream,
The world's great master, and o'er all supreme.
Faithful defender, and the eye of right,
Of steeds the ruler, and of life the light:
With sounding whip four fiery steeds you guide,
When in the glittering car of day you ride,
Propitious on these mystic labours shine,
And bless thy suppliants with a life divine."[19]

(4) Ceremoniously decapitate Prince Charming, saying:

> "Once upon a time
> In a kingdom far away,
> There was a wee pretty prince
> Hoping Prince Charming was on his way.
> But he soon got bored of waiting,
> He dreamed, and yes, he dared
> To pull the head off that fucker

---

[19] Part of The Orphic Hymn To The Sun

And drink from it unimpaired."[20]

(5) Toss your effigy of Prince Charming onto the fire with some frankincense, reserving the gourd-head and filling it with wine. Take a big drink and claim his power for your own.

(6) Continue to dance and drink wine from the "skull" for the rest of the night. Near the end of the ritual, before the fire has died down, toss the decapitated gourd into the fire.

---

[20] I would like to thank my "anxiety-ridden, nut job edit or-in-chief," Shawn Shadow, for helping me with this limerick. If not for his macabre sense of humor and his willingness to indulge me, I would never have come up with so humorous a way to disempower Prince Charming.

2 ADDICTED TO LOVE

Have you ever wondered what Atlas was actually the god of and why he needed to be punished so severely in the Greek myth?

According to Judika Illes in her *Encyclopedia of Spirits*, "Atlas is the Lord of Dangerous Wisdom. He plumbs the depths of the sea. He knows the mysteries of the universe."[21] In some versions of the myth, Atlas is portrayed as gullible. This depiction most likely comes from his role in Hercules' twelve labors where Hercules tricks Atlas into stealing the Golden Apples for him. However, even Homer seems to agree with Illes about the wisdom of this Titan. Homer calls him "deadly-minded" and portrays him as both strong and resilient. He stands just beyond the Western horizon with his feet firmly planted on the ocean floor, holding the sky aloft on his massive shoulders. Regardless of which version you read, his myth does seem to suggest that he understands the mysteries of sea and sky, as Illes describes. How else could he root himself there to hold the sky, his father, from coupling once more with the earth, his mother?

Traditionally, we are told that Atlas was forced to hold up the sky on his shoulders because he led the Titans in their failed war against Zeus. However, the truth is so much more clandestine than all that. There is an occult truth in this myth. Dangerous wisdom, wisdom that runs counter to the establishment or wisdom that frees people from their chains, must bear a heavy burden so that more people don't try to benefit from it or spread it around to others who could thereby become impossible to control.[22]

As fascinating as this revelation about Atlas was when I first read it in Illes's book, it paled in comparison to the realization of what lay at the very heart of the wisdom that we deem to be

---

[21] Illes, Judika. *Encyclopedia of Spirits: the ultimate guide to the magic of fairies, genies, demons, ghosts, gods & goddesses*. Harper One: 2009, p. 229.

[22] This was certainly the case with the wisdom of witchcraft in the dark ages.

"dangerous." For that, we must turn to Atlas's daughter: Calypso.

Calypso, "the dread Goddess with human speech," who is a pre-Olympian goddess of love, beauty, and seduction, stands at the very heart of our question. Think about it for a moment. The Greeks were telling us that seduction and the love that it engenders are born of a dangerous wisdom! If that's true, it begins to make a lot of sense as to why the topic of love terrifies us all so much and why it is so difficult to get a handle on our interactions with each other.

Love is the most dangerous wisdom of all!

That is why it had to be diminished or trivialized, which is where Romanticism and the modern fairy tale come into play. By perpetuating a saccharine version of love, something that made a false version look more appealing than the real thing, people would turn away from real love and the power it holds. They would content themselves with the thrill of the chase and wouldn't strive to connect on a deeper, more meaningful level. Ultimately, this would make them easier to control. In my opinion, this is one of the reasons that witchcraft covens build their bonds off of "acts of love and pleasure." They are the very cornerstones of our faith.

Before any one accuses me of being hyperbolic, antagonistic, or crazy regarding the state of love and the overarching establishment, let me remind you, dear reader, of the point that I made in *Garbed In Green*. Stories about Gay men, like myths about Hercules and Achilles, were repurposed to cast an exclusively heteronormative light on their heroes. These re-writes perpetuated the dichotomy between the sexes while at the same time encouraging both parties to "play their part," or toe the party line.

Take for example the Disney version of Hercules, where his twelve labors were repurposed to be feats of daring-do meant to impress Meg. In the real myth, the labors were atonement for an offense against the gods. These mythic feats weren't some gallant show of strength meant to assail a woman's sexual defenses and get her to fall in love, but Disney, perpetuating the drama of "true love," perverted them towards that new purpose. When the stories couldn't be repurposed with the heteronormative agenda in mind, they were simply eliminated, like the Epic of Gilgamesh.

They certainly weren't going to perpetuate the drama of "true love" for Gay men. The whole point to repurposing these stories for straight couples in the first place was to marginalize and, ultimately, erase Gay men.

Have you ever asked yourself why they needed to do that?

In *Garbed In Green*, I talk about how the Gay male witch is uniquely qualified to be a magical dynamo all by his lonesome. I also talk about the awesome power that can be generated by two fully-functioning Gay male witches uniting in love and sympathy. Is it any wonder why "they" would want to derail our search for real loving partnerships with each other by distracting us with this false romanticism? It is precisely because it disempowers us and keeps us isolated and alone that Gay men must be willing to give up the fantasy and embrace something more realistic.

In order to undo the damage caused by Western Society's homophobia, we must help Gay men reconnect with a more meaningful concept of what a loving partnership ought to look like. These partners must enhance each other's lives, not derail everything into an unholy, chaotic mess, as is so often the case with many current Gay male relationships.

Despite the modern insistence on a prerequisite of sexual attraction and romance, these two requirements are not essential parts of a successful union, Gay or otherwise. Throughout much of human history, love, sex, and romance have had very little to do with each other. Rather the feeling that we call "in love" today was a biological mutation, which helped with the evolution of the species. Nothing more.

During the hunter-gatherer period of human history, when we were nomadic and lived our lives in a flight or fight reality, we did not have the luxury of concerning ourselves with things like romance. Instead, pairings were exclusively about procreation or sexual release. When not using sex as a stress reliever, our hunter-gatherer ancestors only had two things on the sexual agenda: produce as many babies as possible in as short a time as possible and ensure that those babies survived long enough to be useful to the tribe. They instinctively balanced these two goals for the betterment of the tribe.

As we all know, pregnancy is very hard on the mother, and the first two or three years of raising a child can be grueling for the couple. Not much has changed on that front between our hunter-gatherer days and modern times. Our female ancestors were considerably more vulnerable to attack during their pregnancies and after giving birth than their male counterparts. After the delivery, the child was also extremely vulnerable for those first few years of its life.

Nature, recognizing this fact, instilled a biological failsafe in our species to ensure that mother and child were protected during the most vulnerable times in the mating cycle. That failsafe is the feeling that we call being "in love". It made certain that mother and father stayed together long enough to raise the child till it could achieve a modicum of independence (roughly 2-3 years old). Then the "in love" feeling disappeared and the mating couple parted ways to continue to reproduce their genes with other partners.

In truth, the feeling of being in love is nothing more than a hormonal release that lasts anywhere from six months to three years. Does it come as any surprise to you that this timeframe is nearly identical to the period of time that both mother and child are at their most vulnerable? By encouraging the adult male and female partners to have a continued vested interest in each other through this feeling of being in love, Nature ensured that mother and child would have a built-in protector to secure their safety during that extremely vulnerable time.

Today, we have conflated the biological mutation which helped us survive as a species with a requirement for even considering a potential partner. When that "in love" feeling goes away, as it invariably must, we mistakenly believe that our relationships have failed. We break up, abandoning the other person for a "better" option, and start the cycle all over again.

The fact that the "in love" feeling does disappear was equally as essential to our ancestor's survival as the rush of the endorphins in the beginning of their couplings. Without the decrease in these chemicals, the partnerships might have been more lasting and the male's ability to produce more genetic offspring could have been significantly hampered. At that time, humanity needed the advantage of his vast procreative power.

Modern takes on love and romance refuse to acknowledge these simple genetic factors, and we beat ourselves up for our own presumed failures in trying to navigate love as a spiritual or transcendent concept. In our failure to account for biology, we have allowed ourselves to fall victim to a drug addiction of sorts. Many of us approach love from the same perspective as an alcoholic approaches a drink or a heroin addict approaches the needle. We crave the good feeling that comes with the high of each new encounter, and we dread the low that comes when the chemicals inevitably wear off.

On average, Gay men seem to be especially caught up in this vicious cycle in a way that Straight people on average seem at least moderately better-equipped to navigate. For the record, I do not believe that this discrepancy is because there is something deficient in Gay men or superior in the overarching Straight culture. In fact, I actually believe that a huge reason for the handicap Gay men face around issues of love rests with a lack of social infrastructure. Straight culture has significantly more support around issues of love, marriage, and family than the Gay Community. Straight culture also has rites of passage and social pressures that can be applied when men and women refuse to play their parts. The Gay Community has very little support, especially in these areas.

Unable to get an extended supply of this internal chemical release, many Gay men turn instead to self-medicating by introducing external chemicals into their systems. This is, in my opinion, one of the reasons that the Gay Community is plagued by rampant addictions of every variety. I believe that if we could teach Gay men to control their bodies and regulate their endorphins, as the witch does, this need for external chemicals would greatly diminish within our community. More importantly, understanding the balance between the physical, mental, and spiritual aspects of love, sex, and romance in Gay male relationships could also help Gay men attain genuinely satisfying loving relationships with each other.

3 WHAT'S LOVE GOT TO DO WITH IT?

Once we acknowledge that the current state of Gay dating has a problem, we face another more profound dilemma. It's sort of like confronting the scariest set of Russian stacking dolls one has ever seen.

How do we get out of this situation?

Let me recap what I believe the problem to be, as I have laid it out so far. First, we have all been raised to take on the role of the Prince in the fairy tales, which our parents read to us as children. Up until very recently in our society's history, it was very rare that a mother, holding her newborn baby boy in her arms, would consider that he might grow up to be Gay.[23] It was even more rare, perhaps to the point of non-existent, that this mother would actively encourage her son to develop along those lines. Invariably, the majority of us were raised to identify with the male hero or Prince in the stories we were told, and we adopted all of the entitlement and male privilege that comes with that heroic or regal status. Second, because of her glamour and the fact that she gets her man in the end, most romantic Gay men see themselves in Cinderella. This is even true for overtly masculine Gay men who might pass for straight. The role of Cinderella is insidious, and its tendrils creep up in the most unlikely places. Gay men identify with her ambitions and, because of the isolation of the closets, we also identify with the dreadful way that she was treated by her stepmother and stepsisters. This creates what Psychology refers to as cognitive dissonance. Third, unlike straight culture, the Gay Community has no social infrastructure to help navigate these issues.

---

[23] My mom did consider this very fact, by the way ... or so she says. Apparently, she knew by the time I was 6 months old. She credits my love of Dolly Parton (and a few other female singers, but mostly Dolly) with her precognitive insight.

For a starting point on finding answers regarding love between two men, I can think of nowhere better for Gay male witches to turn than to the ancient Greeks. While modern versions of fairy tales leave us with only one unrealistic type of love, the Greeks broke love down into eight diverse forms of expression. In my opinion, the best place to start this discussion of the Greeks is with Plato, because while modern fairy tales land us in a heteronormative construct, Plato generally advocates homosexual sex and love as his defacto position.

In his book, *Plato's Erotic Dialogues*, William S. Cobb says, "In the various views that are expressed about the nature and significance of love in both dialogues, the sexual expression of love that is considered is almost always homosexual in form. Moreover, homosexual relationships are generally approved of by the speakers in the dialogues, although it is recognized that these relationships are sometimes wrong."[24]

When Cobb says that these homosexual relationships are sometimes viewed to be wrong, he is talking about accepted norms and practices within the community of men who sleep with other men at the time. He is not addressing this moral issue from the point-of-view of an outsider's condemnation of these men, like Gay men experience today. One primary example of how a homosexual relationship could be viewed to be wrong in this context is the case where an older man continues to be the receptive partner past a certain age.

Cobb is not talking about homosexuality being wrong from a homophobic or modern Judeo-Christian perspective, which can be seen when he says, "there is nothing improper, abnormal, or immoral about a homosexual relationship as such. In the *Phaedrus* Socrates does express some reservations about the sexual dimension of these relationships, but his remarks are more cautionary than condemnatory and must be interpreted within the context of the dialogue."[25]

---

[24] Cobb, William S. *Plato's Erotic Dialogues*. State University of New York Press, 1993, p. 4.

[25] Cobb, William S. *Plato's Erotic Dialogues*. State University of New York Press, 1993, p. 4.

Personally speaking, I have the same concerns and worries about the overly sexual nature of Gay relationships that Socrates does. We see his predictions running rampant over our community every time we open the hookup apps on our phones. We also see the truth of his wisdom in the fact that any part of the Gay Community that isn't overtly sexual is hidden behind our hyper-sexualized interactions.

In the *Symposium*, Plato has Socrates recount the wisdom he learned from his mentor, Diotima.[26] In his retelling of her theory, Socrates shows Diotima as glorifying the union of two men with each other. From my perspective, this is the most useful aspect of Plato's theories on love, because it touches on the very reason for love outside of biology or physical sex, and Gay men need to hear that at this point in history.

According to Socrates's account of Diotima's wisdom, "mortal nature seeks as far as possible to be eternal and immortal, and it is only in this way, by producing offspring, that it is able to do so."[27] This wisdom stands at the heart of the discussion about how to transcend our biology and begin creating a spiritual version of love that will uplift and enhance the lives of all parties involved.

At the very core of the desire for sex then is a desire to avoid death. For Gay men, who notoriously, prize youth and beauty so highly, this is a very real struggle. If you doubt that this is true, simply look at the sheer number of aging Gay men who battle with what modern psychology has labeled the *Peter Pan Syndrome*.

Because Diotima's philosophy mentions pregnancy, you might be tempted to think that it leaves Gay men out of the equation entirely, but she disabuses us of that misconception when she says, "All human beings are pregnant, Socrates, both in body and in soul, and when we come of age, we naturally desire to give

---

[26] Diotima was an Greek prophetess and philosopher (read: Pagan Priestess) who was said to have taught Socrates all that he knew of wisdom.

[27] Cobb, William S. *Plato's Erotic Dialogues*. State University of New York Press, 1993, p.45, 207d.

birth."[28] Her statement that "All human beings are pregnant" includes men as well as women. She states so plainly in the text. For modern audiences, let me be specific here. It also includes Gay as well as Straight people, Transgender people, and anyone else you might want to highlight for consideration. It is a natural condition of the entire human experience (not just the female experience) in her theory, that "when we come of age, we naturally desire to give birth." This desire to give birth is a desire to leave something lasting, something that survives our own death to the world that will allow us to achieve some small measure of immortality.

"Now, those who are pregnant in body are more oriented toward women and are lovers in that way, providing immortality, remembrance, and happiness for themselves for all time, as they believe, by producing children."[29] According to Diotima, this seems to be the strategy that Straight people, specifically Straight men, apply towards achieving immortality. Ignoring the misogynistic undertones in this recounting (Plato certainly has been read as having some misogynistic issues to work out), Diotima's wisdom seems sound. From a purely evolutionary perspective, it does make sense. Every organism seeks to reproduce itself, to pass on its best genes to the next generation, and by doing so, live on eternally. We discussed a version of this earlier in connection with the "in love" feeling and its function in helping our hunter-gather ancestors rear their offspring.

"'Those who are pregnant in soul however—for there are people who are even more pregnant in their souls than in their bodies,' she continued, 'these people are pregnant with and give birth to what is appropriate for the soul.'"[30] Good sense, virtue, judiciousness, and justice are some of the things with which these

---

[28] Cobb, William S. *Plato's Erotic Dialogues*. State University of New York Press, 1993, p.44, 206c.

[29] Cobb, William S. *Plato's Erotic Dialogues*. State University of New York Press, 1993, p.46, 208e.

[30] Cobb, William S. *Plato's Erotic Dialogues*. State University of New York Press, 1993, p.46, 208e-209a.

people are said to be pregnant. As Diotima reveals this list, it becomes apparent that the people who are pregnant in soul give birth to mental things—thoughts, theories, strategy, works of art and literature.[31]

That Diotima ascribes this type of pregnancy as existing most often between men who love other men is clear in the text. "Whenever someone who has been pregnant in his soul with these things from youth, and who is reaching adulthood and coming into his prime, desires to give birth and produce offspring, he goes around, I believe, searching for something beautiful, with which he can produce offspring. He can never produce offspring with something that is ugly. Hence, since he is pregnant with these things, he eagerly embraces beautiful bodies rather than ugly ones, and should he happen upon someone who has a beautiful, well-bred, and naturally gifted soul as well, he embraces the combination with great enthusiasm and immediately engages in many conversations with this man about virtue, about what a good man should be like, and what he should make it his business to do; thus, he sets out to educate him. When he attaches himself to someone beautiful, I believe, and associates with him, he gives birth and brings forth what he was pregnant with before, both while in that person's presence and while remembering him when he's absent."[32]

Though it has been convention in much of the English language's history to use the masculine pronoun *he* when referring to people in general, the use of *he* and *him* in this translation of Plato's original Greek is not participating in that convention. That Diotima is actually referring to the love between two men (people we would refer to as *Gay, Queer, Homosexual,* etc. today) can be seen when she says: "and should **he** happen upon someone who

---

[31] As a side note, this conception of the *soul* as *mind* is very common even to our modern Western occult perspective by the way. The older occultists looked at the human soul from this exact perspective. They viewed the spirit as the reincarnating thing, the soul as a mind of sorts, and the body as the physical vehicle connected to the other two. It has only been in recent decades that we have confused the soul and the spirit.

[32] Cobb, William S. *Plato's Erotic Dialogues*. State University of New York Press, 1993, p.46, 209b-209c.

has a beautiful, well-bred, and naturally gifted soul as well, **he** embraces the combination with great enthusiasm and immediately engages in many conversations with this **man** ...". In several places in this dialogue, Socrates recounts Diotima speaking about *people*, *women*, and countless other inclusive terms to identify the exact type of person she is talking about. The fact that Diotima chooses to talk specifically about the coupling using the exclusive terms *he* and *man* here in relation to each other instead of choosing more inclusive terms in this instance certainly seems to imply a homosexual union, especially when considered against the knowledge that unions between men in this way were a common practice during his time. Remember what Cobb said earlier in this chapter, that Plato's de facto position on issues of love was homosexual. This is one of those cases in the text.

Aleister Crowley came up with a similar theory in the modern era. In his book *Gay Witchcraft: Empowering the Tribe*, Christopher Penczak recounts Crowley's theory: "whereas heterosexual relationships help keep the cycles of life going in the physical plane, homosexual relationships—not directing their energy to physical conception—directs energy to magical pursuits, perhaps continuing the life cycles of the magical realms, such as the collective unconscious."[33] What Penczak refers to as "magical pursuits" and the sustenance of the "magical realms" in this instance would be considered by Plato to be qualities of the soul in that they are mental or psychic powers. Plato, Crowley, and Penczak each recognize the innate power of Gay male unions in their own ways, and none of them make any bones about it.

In fact, there is no shortage of material on the subject of Gay male relationships and the power that they produce for one who wishes to dive deeper into the literature. I discuss this topic in more depth in my previous book, *Garbed In Green*. Pulling from material laid out by Gavin and Yvonne Frost and their study of occult anatomy, I talk about how all Gay men can generate great magical power individually and how two Gay men, united in

---

[33] Penczak, Christopher. *Gay Witchcraft: Empowering the Tribe*. Red Wheel/Weiser, LLC, 2003, p. 65-66.

bonds of love and sympathy, can generate exponentially more power together.[34]

Pair-bonded relationships between men were prized for more than just the power they could produce in the ancient world. They made the two participants immortal in the eyes of all who witnessed their union. Granted, Achilles shook the earth over the death of Patroclus and Gilgamesh and Enkidu were an unstoppable force together, but the real allure of these potent relationships was the potential for granting the two partners some small measure of immortality.

In the *Symposium*, Diotima says as much about the union of two men when she says "Everyone would prefer to bring forth this sort of children[35] rather than human offspring. People are envious of Homer, Hesiod, and the other good poets because of the offspring they left behind, since these are the sort of offspring that, being immortal themselves, provide their procreators with an immortal glory and an immortal remembrance."[36]

As wonderful as Gay sex can be, it is not enough to make the magic happen. Sex is merely one piece of the puzzle, not the whole picture. In order to engage the full power (magical or otherwise) available between two men in union with each other, there must be more than just lust and sex driving the bonding. In order for the full potential to be achieved, the two men must be in sympathy with each other on a deeper level. Yes, the physical desire is important, but so is being of the same mind or uniting the wills towards a common goal. These things cannot be minimized or overlooked simply because they are inconvenient or we are lonely, insecure, or afraid. Whereas the product of Straight unions is a biological offspring, this is never the case for Gay male relationships without scientific intervention. Rather, the product of our unions, the piece that will grant us the immortality Diotima

---

[34] Giovinco, Casey. *Garbed In Green: Gay Witchcraft & The Male Mysteries.* Publisher: Casey Giovinco, 2018, p. 45-49.

[35] The "children" that Diotima is referring to here are what some today have jokingly called "thought babies."

[36] Cobb, William S. *Plato's Erotic Dialogues.* State University of New York Press, 1993, p.47, 209d

talks about, and mitigate the Peter Pan Syndrome that psychology studies, requires us to engage the soul (or mind, in modern lingo) as well as the body, because, as Diotima said, the byproduct of our unions belongs to the quality of the soul.

Some versions of Initiatory Witchcraft, like Gala, hold a similar concept about being in sympathy with each other. This concept stands at the center of their mysteries. It is upon these individual mysteries that these traditions build their own unique initiations. The phrase *Perfect Love and Perfect Trust,* which is commonly batted about in the various magical communities today, stands as a key part in this process of getting the initiator and initiate into sympathy with each other on a deeper level. This profoundly deep bond is essential for the branches of Witchcraft that initiate in this manner.

Whether you are talking about finding a partner or initiating into a traditional coven, however, issues of love and sex invariably come up. For Gay men who want more than just a hookup or a "friends with benefits" situation, this discussion is essential.[37] For Gay male neophytes, who desire to join a coven within any of the branches of Initiatory Witchcraft that initiate using the Perfect Love and Perfect Trust model, having the ability to genuinely love yourself and others is also essential. Unfortunately, our closets, our training within the most visible parts of the Gay Community, and the sense of isolation that a great many Gay men feel when they don't fit in to the Gay Standard, does nothing to help prepare them for finding a loving partner or joining one of these traditional covens.

Fortunately, the value of ancient Greece's legacy for modern

---

[37] For Gay men who are currently feeling fulfilled by their experiences within the traditional Gay sex scene of the bars and clubs or the hookup apps, this information may fall on deaf ears, and these individuals may simply put this book down. Another possibility is that this philosophy may be so unpopular with these people that it causes some of them to be genuinely angry with me, this book, or even the world. I am prepared to accept any of those outcomes, because the potential to help Gay men who want a genuine connection with each other is just too great to worry about the ones who want to continue to engage in the other avenues of self-expression.

Gay men does not stop with Plato and Diotima's immortality theory. That is merely the beginning. The ancient Greeks actually had a more robust understanding of love than we currently do, and we can use it to alleviate a great deal of our own current struggles in loving ourselves and each other.

The ancient Greeks recognized eight different kinds of love, and they spent a great deal of time detailing how these versions of love affected humanity. They even talked about how one should go about engaging in the various styles of love. Aristotle, Plato's student, wrote a book where he investigated **Philia** (brotherly love).[38] That book was one of his mostly widely influential works.

Most people today know about **eros** (or erotic love) and philia, but few people realize that there are six more versions of love left to explore. Our options are not just erotic lust or the "friend zone." We could also experience the playful love that is often associated with flirting (**ludus**), or, depending on the circumstances and the state of mind of the participants, the playfulness of ludus can turn obsessive and **mania** can take hold.[39] Conversely, we might experience the long-standing love typically associated with committed relationships (**pragma**). It is this style of love that we so often hear about when people say that you have to prioritize the traits and circumstances that you label as *non-negotiable* and compromise on the negotiable qualities so that you can achieve a lasting union. Like pragma, **storge** is a lasting and enduring love. It is often translated as *familial love*, and it is most often used to represent the type of devotion that a parent has for a child. The Greeks even recognized a love of self (**philautia**), which is all too lacking in our modern world. This is not the arrogance or brashness associated with someone who is self-obsessed.[40] Instead this type of love belongs to the person who

---

[38] Aristotle devotes two books of his *Nicomachean Ethics* to investigating the topic of philia.

[39] While ludus and mania are not directly connected in any systematic way, it is all-too-easy for lovers to transition from ludus into mania.

[40] That might be considered a type of mania.

truly knows himself, the person who has found his place in this world.[41] Finally, there is **agape**, which, despite Christian misappropriation, is so essential for witches. It is the type of love that we have for our Horned God and Great Mother Goddess and it serves as the foundation for perfect love and perfect trust when used in initiatory covens.

For Gay men, the value of breaking down our modern concept of love in a similar way to the way the ancient Greeks did is immeasurable. It will go a long way towards preventing the negative thoughts around loneliness that many Gay men have. One of the reasons that so many men are so lonely today is that they live in a lack mentality around issues of love. It is either erotic love, flirtation with the hope of getting erotic love, full-on commitment, or nothing at all! The truth is that the negative thoughts of a large swath of Gay men in the Gay Community are actually indicative of a supreme lack mentality around issues of love.

Whenever we have a lack mentality, our minds are operating in a negative current. For the sake of visualization purposes, we might conceptualize this in a simplified manner. Imagine your thoughts are whirling around in your head in a widdershins (or counter-clockwise) direction whenever you think negatively. As witches, we know that when we cast our circles widdershins, we are taking advantage of the negative energetic current or the magnetic forces and drawing things to us.

Having this information is not the same as putting it to use. It's all well-and-good to talk about appreciating the various styles of love and keeping a positive attitude while you enjoy the experiences you have with other men, but if the body is screaming out to get its sexual needs met, very little else is going to register until the urges have been dealt with or silenced.

Let's address that concern now by creating an elemental servitor to help us alleviate our doubt and worry and then we can continue on with the theory portion of our journey.

---

[41] Sybil Leek once said that the most powerful spell a witch could cast was to find his place in the world. This type of love is the foundation upon which that spell is built.

4 A THOUGHTFORM ELEMENTAL SERVITOR

In his book *The Occult World*, Alfred Percy Sinnett says, "Every thought of man upon being evolved passes into another world, and becomes an active entity by associating itself, coalescing we might term it, with an elemental—that is to say, with one of the semi-intelligent forces of the kingdoms. It survives as an active intelligence—a creature of the mind's begetting—for a longer or shorter period proportionate with the original intensity of the cerebral action which generated it."[42]

Sinnett goes on to say that most of us are continuously overpopulating our individual worlds with these "offsprings of fancies, desires, impulses, and passions." They cluster around us like passengers on a crowded New York subway car, creating a frenetic or chaotic jumble in our minds and the minds of anyone else unfortunate enough to come in contact with them. Even the most wonderful of these entities (say for example a thought of success) can cause great havoc simply by existing side-by-side with the various other thoughts you think on a regular basis.

This is one of the reasons why meditation is universally viewed to be a staple of any reputable spiritual system. It quiets the mind and prevents the haphazard creation of these thought entities (we witches call them *thoughtform elementals* or just *thoughtforms*). The real difference between an adept witch and a novice rests with the ability to control the mind through meditation.

For the record, that little wisdom has nothing to do with the trite, simple platitude that everyone always spouts around meditation. It's not just about controlling one's thoughts. On the one hand, meditation, as the witch sees it, is about training the mind to disempower and let go of unnecessary thoughts with the ultimate goal of clearing one's mental space of the clutter. By

---

[42] Sinnett, A. P. *The Occult World. Trübner & Co., 1889, 89-90.*

releasing these unwanted thoughts and refusing to dwell on them, the witch cuts off the associated thoughtform's ability to continue to influence him. It really is as simple as that: turn your attention away from a thought long enough, refuse to turn back to it, and, eventually, it will lose its power over you, or it will go on to someone else with less control over his own mind. On the other hand, meditation, as the witch sees it, is also about learning how to purposefully and intentionally create these entities for the individual witch's own betterment. The witch allows these desired thoughtforms to exist within his mental space so long as they are useful to him, and then he releases them once they have done their intended work.[43]

That is exactly what we are going to do here in this exercise: create a specific thoughtform to serve you in your quest for finding the love you desire. However, for this exercise to work, you must become like the adept witch. You must be willing to meditate and to turn inward to find your own strength and power.

Before we begin, it is worth noting that this Thoughtform is going to do its work ON YOU. You are not sending it off to influence someone else—specific or otherwise. The entire purpose of this spell is to get YOU ready for the next step in the process of finding a loving partner. While there are certainly many versions of love, and this spell does account for them all (monogamy, polyamory, open relationship, etc.), it is not designed to get you laid. Rather, it's designed to get you ready for a committed, healthy relationship however you are choosing to define that for yourself at this time.

Before you can effectively create a thoughtform to act as a Servitor for you, however, you must eliminate all doubt and fear of failure. These things are contrary to your goal of finding a loving partner, and they will only crowd your consciousness, making it harder for the chosen thoughtform to influence you.

Undoubtedly, you've heard people say: "I can't meditate." The reason they "can't meditate" is because their minds are so cluttered with these errant thoughtforms. They are constantly

---

[43] It should go without saying that the wise witch also refrains from creating too many of these entities at once, especially if they are in conflict with one another.

being pulled in opposing directions by these unseen forces, and they barely have the time or space to breathe, let alone achieve their heart's desires.

Should you wish to overcome this "inability to meditate," simply turn your attention away from all thoughts that are contrary to your desired goal. In doing so, you must clear your mind of all but that desired thought. I know. That is often easier said than done.

When talking to witches in Gala, I constantly joke about my mentor failing to explain stuff to me that he felt was simple. I would be in awe of the magical feats he was able to perform, and I would ask him how he did it. Invariably, he would respond with, "You just do."

His answer infuriated me so much at the time. I knew he didn't "just do it." I knew in my heart that there were steps he took to "just do it," but he either stubbornly refused to reveal those intermediary steps or he was actually so good at magic that he didn't think about them.

Looking back on it now, I am so grateful to my mentor for taking that approach with my training. It forced me to explore, to research, and to experiment. In many ways, his infuriatingly simple response started me down the path that led to writing this *Gay Witchcraft & The Male Mysteries* series of books. In truth, and as frustrating as it was at the time, I wouldn't change his answer for the world. It taught me much more than I would have learned had he spoon-fed me the wisdom.

Very few people appreciate the transformative power of frustration the way that most of the initiated witches I know do. Instead, frustration seems to be a stumbling block that derails most people. So, because I have no desire to derail your progress towards finding the love you desire, I am going to break down the process that will lead to success in overcoming this hurdle.

For the next two weeks (two weeks at least—it may take longer), take a mental inventory of your current thoughts and the thought processes that you experience daily. If you are not already engaged in a regular journaling practice, now would be an excellent time to start. Journaling is immensely useful in getting to know yourself as well as training the mind.

Once you determine which thoughts dominate your mind,

which hopes and ambitions drive you, which fears control you, it is time to begin denying and releasing the negative ones. This is where a regular meditation practice will begin to pay off.[44] By meditating consistently, you will begin to observe that you are not your thoughts. You will also release attachment to those thoughts. You will be able to recognize the positive or negative value of each independent thought that acts on you, and you will be able to empower the good and disempower the bad.

In the process of denying and releasing the unwanted and intrusive thoughts, there are several techniques that will help. If the thought is fleeting, like "I really should be doing the laundry," simply swipe left in your mind's eye and lay a red opaque lens over the thought before it disappears, like you're on Tinder. The opaque red filter will stop the thought and eliminate it from your consciousness. If the intruding thought is actually one you need to remember and act on later, swipe right and see a green transparent lens appear over it. Let that indicate that you will remember it after your meditation session is over.[45]

For some of the more powerful thoughts that intrude on your conscious awareness, it may be necessary to engage a more active imaginative technique. Picture the dominating thoughts as balloons in your mind's eye. See them floating up into a clear blue sky. If they refuse to float away, imagine an appropriate gust of wind to help them along. If they still refuse to leave you after that, imagine popping that damn balloon in some way. If you're into archery, fire an arrow at it. Use your imagination on this one. Make it fun for yourself. Distract yourself with the joy of popping the balloon.

And, if that is still not enough, you may have to engage the concept of *occult denial*. My mentor always told me that occult denials are a form of occult statement, which have a most positive effect when used correctly. First, focus your Will. Steal yourself

---

[44] If you do not already have a meditation practice. You can find a basic structure for one outlined in my previous book *Garbed In Green*. The value of meditation can never be overstated.

[45] As brilliant as this technique is, I really can't take credit for it. My mentor gave it to me and a few other Gala witches at our last Grand Coven. I thought it was so brilliant that I had to include it here for you.

against the dominating thought. Boldly deny the obstacle or difficulty which besets your path. Deny it right out of existence. For example, if you were struggling with feelings of loneliness, you might say, "I DENY loneliness. Loneliness has no power over me. I deny it out of my world. For me, it does NOT exist." Make your denials into positive commands. Do not beg. Don't be wishy-washy. Be resolute and firm in your command, and believe its truth completely.

I have also found that following up an occult denial with a complementary affirmation helps. For example, if you were trying to ditch your feelings of loneliness and the occult denial alone wasn't sufficient to overcome that obstacle, you might say something like, "I make friends easily and effortlessly" or "I always have companionship available to me."

Once you have eliminated and denied all the obstacles standing in your way of achieving a peaceful mental state, it is time to begin the next part of the process. Don't worry if that peaceful mental state only stays peaceful for five to ten minutes. That's more than enough time to cast the spell. You can work on prolonging that state later if you desire.

Begin thinking about what you actually want in a relationship at this time. Do you just want a boyfriend or even a more long-term partner? Maybe you're poly and you want several partners? Any and all of these are wonderful. What type of companionship are you looking for?

Regardless of which type of companionship you desire, it is important to begin better understanding your own needs in this relationship. You've already spent two weeks preparing your mind for this. Take another two weeks (or more if you need it) and uncover what you really want at this time. Don't rush the process, and don't waste your time fantasizing about what you want your partner to look like or how you want him to behave. Focus on yourself and what you need to change about YOU to succeed in this process.

If you want a boyfriend, what things about yourself have been standing in your way up to this point? I know that it is easy to just profess that Gay men are shallow, unnecessarily harsh, or simply not interested in relationships, but that's not entirely the case. Yes, Gay dating is hard, and yes, Gay men are all those things that I just listed, but Gay men are also wonderful, kind, caring, and compassionate people. If you are failing to run into someone who fits into the latter categories, it is because you are closed off to it and can't see it in some way.

I know that's harsh, and I know it's not what you want to hear; but, if I pander to your fears and insecurities, we will never get you what you really want. So, if you really do want a fulfilling relationship, let go of your past experiences with Gay men. Let go of your belief that you need to influence someone else in any way at this time, and instead, take a good, hard look at yourself.

Be honest about your shortcomings. Were you needy in the past? How about insecure? Did horniness get in the way of previous connections? Do you have shame or guilt—either unconscious, or unspoken, or even blatant?

Look at all of those things and more. Really get a feel for the part you played in your past experiences with men and accept the reality of it. Don't sugarcoat anything for yourself. It will only delay your success. You can find guidelines for doing this in the Personal Inventory section of *Garbed In Green*, or, if you're familiar with Alcoholics Anonymous, you can implement their advice for doing a Fourth Step.[46]

Let's use me as an example. I have always wanted to be married. For me, dating was never enough. If the guy didn't express an interest in marriage early on, I wasn't interested in even going out on another date with him. I remember one first date where I actually asked the guy what his ideas around marriage were. I also said very matter-of-factly on that date that "If you're not interested in marriage, there's no reason to order dessert." (I was truly fed up with being single at that point, and I saw every new encounter as a waste of my time or a delay of my ultimate agenda if it wasn't going to lead to a proposal.) Needless-to-say, I

---

[46] Personally speaking, I am not an alcoholic, but I have found great occult wisdom in several aspects of their program. The Fourth Step is one such place. Don't let the label of "alcoholic" keep you from fully benefiting from the universal occult truth behind this personal inventory process. If you have questions about how to do this effectively, begin your research by picking up a copy of their "Big Book." It is actually titled Alcoholics Anonymous, and I have included its bibliographical information in this book's list of resources.

came off a little "intense," and I may have scared a great many good guys away. My own insecurities around not being good enough got the better of me, and I just wanted one man to validate my worth to him. That level of desperation was a huge turn off, and I must concede that, because I indulged that side of myself instead of fixing my own damage, I contributed to my own status as a single Gay man.

What insecurities, fears, doubts, frustrations, anger, pain, guilt, shame, etc. do you have that is like that? What are you holding onto so tightly that you're squeezing the life out of it? What do you refuse to compromise on?

These are the questions you must ask yourself, and you must be willing to hear the answers from your higher, objective self. You also must be willing to release them and to fix the broken situations you find yourself in. If you're not willing to do any of this yet, the sad truth is that you may not be ready for the love you say want, and that's okay.

Continue reading through this book without doing the exercises and rituals yet. Just reading it may help. If not, maybe there's something else you need to do for yourself first before you can fully take advantage of the information laid out here. Do that first and then come back to this material when you're ready.

Once you are ready and you have identified the part you played in keeping yourself single when you didn't want to be, it is time to think about creating a thoughtform to serve you in the background of your consciousness, helping to guide those potential mates into your life. Remember though, the meditation, the occult denials, and the affirmations are really important. If you don't do them and you skip right to the construction of the thoughtform servitor, you run the risk of getting either everything you have always gotten in the past, or of the spell simply not working because your own baggage gets in the way again.

Creation of a Thoughtform Elemental Servitor

The process for creating the servitor is actually quite easy. This exercise invokes the spirit of the swan, because swans are said to mate for life and we are looking for a long-term partner or partners in this spell. Should you want to work with less permanent energy, simply find another animal that mates more appropriately to the style of love you are looking to manifest, and let your servitor take that shape. The actual shape itself is not important. What is important is that you give it a shape to control it and that the shape you choose communicates the desired intention to your subconscious every time you interact with it.

When you are ready to call forth your servitor from the astral light, set aside some time on a **Friday night** in an appropriate moon phase. For starting fresh, work at the New Moon. To bring something to you, work during the Waxing Moon. If you want to bring something to a head or increase its power, work at the Full Moon, and if you want to remove an obstacle, which obstructs your path, work during the Waning Moon. Lock the doors on your chosen night and put your phone on silent. Then anoint a **pink candle** with a love drawing oil made from **Orris Root** and **Sandalwood** in a base of either **jojoba** or **apricot** oil. Anoint the candle from the wick to the center. Then repeat the process, moving from the base to the center. Make sure to cover all sides of the candle in your love oil, and as you do this, say a charm, chant, or affirmation appropriate to your purpose. You can find one someone else wrote or come up with one for yourself. Other than concentration and an appropriate brass candlestick, this is all you'll need.

Sit before the pink candle and quiet your mind. Take several slow, deep breaths, making the inhale and exhale equal in length. Eliminate all thoughts from your mind. Sit with a blank, empty mind for a moment or two, like you have been practicing for the last month or so.[47] When you have reached a state of inner peace, conjure up thoughts of love. Don't just think about love though. Really feel it. Remember the last time you felt truly loved. This doesn't have to be romantic love. Any feeling of uplifting love will do for this. What's important is that you actually feel loved. It will raise your vibration.

Open your eyes and light the candle.

Stare into the candle flame. Let it dance. See it split from one flame into two or more. Let it mesmerize you. As you stare into

---

[47] If you have yet to achieve the ability to hold an empty mind for at least two minutes, continue practicing meditation till you succeed with this skill. There is a natural progression for this in Franz Bardon's *Initiation Into Hermetics*.

the center of the flame, see the outline of a grayish orb. See it growing in size until it is floating in 3D above the candle flame in front of you. Now see the orb begin to change color into a beautiful emerald green sphere with a vibrant pink center. As the flame licks the bottom of the sphere, see it pulsate in unison with your breath and grow in size with each exhale. Continue focusing on this imagery until the sphere is at least three feet in diameter.

Now, see the pink center expand out, replacing the emerald green, as if the heat of the color pink were "warming up" the entire sphere. Eventually that sphere burns so hot that the pink becomes dazzling white, producing a glare like the noonday sun. Don't just see it. Feel that heat. Experience every sensation you can in this moment. Exercise the full scope of your witchy imagination.

As the glare dies down, see the sphere morph into the shape of a swan (or whatever animal you chose). See it as clearly as if you were looking at a real swan. Then name it and tell it what you want it to do for you.

In my case, I asked the swan to help me overcome my insecurities around marriage and winding up old and alone. I knew that this was the biggest roadblock to my magical success in this area, and I knew that I needed to eliminate it from my consciousness as quickly as possible. I also knew that the servitor technique was an excellent method of achieving the desired result, because it could work tirelessly in the background until success had been achieved.

The order that you give your servitor must contain the effect it should trigger, stated in the present tense. Think of it like a commanding affirmation. A good command might be: "With your help (swan name), I am a confident married man. Take all doubt and insecurity far from me."

Finally, don't forget to release the servitor back into the astral from whence it came. You can give it a command to dissolve in three months or "when its work is done." That is certainly possible, but I have always felt that it is better to take a stronger hand in these matters and actually go through the effort of deconstructing and releasing my thoughtforms. If you agree with my perspective on this, simply anoint another pink candle at the designated time, and reverse the imagery. Start with the Swan. See it disappear in a dazzling white light. See that light cool back to a brilliant pink color. See the pink aura pulsate, decreasing in size as you breathe in until the emerald green boarder reappears in your sphere. Only the center should remain pink, as it was previously. Then see the sphere shrink in size, turning hazy gray again. Watch as the tiny orb descends back into the center of the flame, then command your swan (stating its name) to return back to the astral light from whence it came. Blow out the candle and repeat the process again for some other obstacle if needed.

5 SELF-LOVE ... AND I DON'T JUST MEAN MASTURBATION!

It was the first of September. My lease was up, and I had yet to find a new place to live. The truth was, I hadn't even started looking, which, despite being out of character for me (a Cancerian male who is all about hearth and home), really wasn't that big of a problem. My mom was out of the country for three weeks, so I spent the intermittent period watching her house.

I had pretty much made up my mind that I wanted to move back down to North Carolina, and two of the Gala witches who lived down there were nice enough to let me stay at their place while I searched for my new home. However, they were traveling and wouldn't be back until the tenth.

So, I had ten days to occupy with writing in solitude. I had just spent the last two years living with a boyfriend and roommates. I still loved him, and I enjoyed living with the roommates, but I was thrilled to have a space to myself again. I wrote during the day, and most nights, I enjoyed a glass of wine and a magical bath.

On the 6th of September, I took a break from the writing to go promote my book. First stop on what I was jokingly calling my "Rainbow Tour" (like I was some modern day Gay male Evita) was a delightfully elegant Victorian Gothic candle shop in Claymont, Delaware called *The Candle Parlour*. I had met the proprietor, Charlie, on Grindr, and we struck up a conversation about Paganism and the occult. At first, I was taken aback that he was genuinely interested in me as a person and not just looking for a hook up, but I am very public about being a witch on my Grindr profile, and there are so few openly spiritual men, let alone openly Pagan guys, on hook up apps. I guess I really shouldn't have been surprised.

As a brief aside, who would have thought that a Gay hook up app would have been so good for something as intellectual and spiritual as a book on witchcraft, Gay or otherwise? Before writing *Garbed In Green*, my Grindr experience consisted of people using dick pics as an alternative form of saying "hello" and conversations that went nowhere because someone (usually me) got uppity.

It never ceases to surprise me how Gay men genuinely seem to think that there should be a different set of rules for us than there are for straight people when it comes to sex and relationships. Although, I should know better by now!

Science has already proven that an increase in testosterone also increases aggressive tendencies. The lack of a female, or a significant feminine influence, in the equation decidedly tips the scales in favor of the testosterone-powered locomotive that is the male procreative drive. That, combined with the oppression that we, as Gay men, suffer from mainstream society, creates a perfect storm that allows dismissive and abusive behaviors to run rampant within Gay hook up culture.

That little hook up app was surprisingly good for my first book. About a good one-third of my second quarter book sales that first year came from men failing to hook up with me off of Grindr. The way it seemed to work was that a guy would ask me to hook up, and I would politely turn him down or ask for a rain check because I had to work. Invariably, he would ask what I did for a living, and when I told him that I wrote books on witchcraft for Gay men, he would express an interest in learning more about my writing. More often than not, these guys would purchase *Garbed In Green* from Amazon and then write me back a few weeks later and tell me how much it spoke to them.

I had some of the most profound discussions since my post-graduate study in applied ethics with some of those men on Grindr after they read my book. They questioned my assumptions. They called me on my biases, but they also asked for further clarification, expressed similar frustrations about dating other men who love men, and talked about how *Garbed In Green* changed the way they approach other men.

As surprised as I was to find this caliber of intelligent discussion and genuine connection on Grindr, I was even more surprised to see that the connection carried over into my face-to-face meeting with Charlie. He had invited me to check out his shop, and I had promised to do so before I went down to North Carolina.

I'll confess: I was worried about meeting him. What if it didn't go well? What if he expected a hook up to occur, and he got vindictive or catty because he was let down? So many thoughts raced through my head, and I almost cancelled our appointment because of fear. Fortunately, the possibility that his shop would carry my book, or we would build a mutually beneficial professional relationship in some other way, was too great to pass up, and I pushed through my discomfort.

The truth is that I genuinely had nothing to worry about. Charlie was a perfect gentleman. Like his shop, Charlie embodied the elegance and charm of a bygone era fused with a thoroughly modern style.

I enjoyed the shop and the company, and whenever I am back in the Philadelphia area, I try to make it a point to buy some products from his shop. Though it is called *The Candle Parlour*, my all-time favorite product he sells is a perfume fragrance called *Blasphemy*. It's absolutely sinful! If you get the chance, buy it from him. You'll be glad you did.

After I left Charlie, I drove the half hour back to Philadelphia's Gayborhood to see if I could meet with the manager of Giovanni's Room and talk about getting them to sell my book. Giovanni's Room is the oldest Gay bookstore in the United States, but, that's not what made me want to get my book onto their shelves. For me, that beautiful little store is so much more than just a national landmark. It's a magical place, a haven.

As a young Gay boy, grappling with my own closet, Giovanni's Room was a safe space where I could go, get a good book, and watch other Gay men living their lives. Though many men "checked me out" back then, I never approached any of them. I was too shy and too insecure. That said, being in that store gave me hope that when I finally did come out of the closet, I would be happy, like they appeared to be.

The first book that I ever bought from there was the book that gave the store its name: *Giovanni's Room* by James Baldwin. In the book, a Gay American expatriate falls in love with a beautiful Bartender named Giovanni. His love for this bartender forces him to confront his desires in contrast to the conventional 1950s morality and face the inevitable weight of his decisions. There is nothing that earmarks this masterpiece as a particularly Gay work of fiction other than the fact that two men love each other and face the human condition within themselves because of that love. It was the first book that I ever read where the book was labeled *Gay*, and it wasn't actually pornography. In my opinion, it is what all "Gay fiction" should be: a work of art that every human being can learn something from, regardless of sexual orientation.

I don't have a problem with porn, but I don't enjoy the fact that everything, which bears the label *Gay*, has to descend into pornography. Let's leave open the possibility that the label might be useful in helping us explore other aspects of the Gay male experience, other than just sex.

James Baldwin taught me that being Gay didn't mean that I had to be content to be relegated to the sidelines in the game of life. I could hold my head up high and be proud of my Gayness. In fact, my Gay Culture could stand side by side and even be considered just as valuable as Black or Jewish Culture in American literature. For me, James Baldwin was as powerful a writer as Toni Morrison or J. D. Salinger. That was an empowering thought for the outcast teenager cowering in the closet.

In truth, I half-expected Giovanni's Room to turn me down. I thought I would have a battle on my hands convincing them to take a look at my book. I'm not sure if I was worried about them being non-witches and it being a controversial topic to the general public or if I held them in such high-regard that I couldn't imagine my book associated with that wonderful store. Perhaps it was a bit of both. I do know that I prepared some counter-arguments to any objections that they might have regarding selling a book on witchcraft, but, fortunately, I didn't need any of them.

Alan, the manager (and buyer) for the store, happened to love my book and think it was a perfect addition to their stock. He actually bought two copies before I even left the store.

The weight of this accomplishment suddenly hit me. I would now be on the same shelves as James Baldwin in the bookstore where I first bought his book! I politely, but very quickly (so that I didn't ruin my reputation by geeking out in front of Alan), said my goodbyes and walked down the street to a local café to have a celebratory lunch. I wanted something extravagant and "hipstery." I had worked hard, and I wanted to enjoy the fruits of my labor. I went to *Tria*, an amazing wine, cheese, and beer bar, and asked for a table for one from the host.

The hot bartender who was soon-to-be my server intervened. "Put him in my section. Nobody that cute should eat alone!"

I generally try not to let stuff like that go to my head. After all, he makes his money from tips. Plus, the café, which was in the heart of Philadelphia's Gayborhood, was practically empty. It was the middle of the afternoon, and it was a safe assumption that any customer walking in off the street would be sexually interested in him.

He was 6'4 and looked to be about 195 pounds of solid muscle. He had the most piercing cornflower blue eyes I have ever seen, which looked even more dramatic against his dark black eyelashes and his perfectly sculpted black eyebrows. Of course he flirted for better tips! I had to keep reminding myself of that as I got lost in those eyes, but all of a sudden, he did something that really threw me off my game.

He invited his friends over to meet "the writer."

"This is Casey," he said to them as they sat around the table, "he just got his book into Giovanni's Room."

They were all immediately interested.

"Ooooh a writer!"

"How exciting!"

"Brilliant and sexy!"

Each of them looked just as good as the one before. It was as if the gods had smiled on me that day. Everything was going my way. I'm not sure what it is about publishing a book that immediately "ups" your sexiness quotient, but publishing a book certainly does seem to do that.

We talked for the better part of two hours, as we leisurely enjoyed an epicurean feast together. The red wine was rich and robust. It coated my mouth like butter. (I know that's not a normal description of red wine, but it's how it felt.) In fact, to this day, I am constantly let down by various different reds, because I compare them to that one. For me, it has become the quintessential experience of drinking red wine. Not only was it the best red wine that I have ever had, it seemed to pair perfectly with everything we ate. Warm poached black missionary figs stuffed with gorgonzola, parmesan, and prosciutto for an appetizer. A truffled mushroom panino with fontina cheese, lemon, spinach, and thyme for the main course, and decadent chocolate torte for dessert.

As amazing as the food was, the company really did kick it up a notch. Isn't that always the case though? While I hate how "Christian" it sounds, I truly believe in the power of breaking bread together. We talked about my book and my theory that the big problem in the Gay Community is that, as a community, we suffer from a chronic case of what the French would call *ennui* or the Germans would call *weltschmerz*. (The English word *angst* really just doesn't seem to do the condition justice.) We talked about how the obsession with the bar scene, hook up culture, and drugs are really just misplaced desires to touch the ecstatic in a vain attempt to reach the magical. That attempt is only vain, by the way, because Western Society has done such a thorough job of telling us that there is no such thing as "magic" since we were children. For magical people (as I believe Gay men are[48]), that convenient lie, which the rest of society has collectively bought into, is truly damaging.

I was genuinely surprised that a group of guys that pretty were held in thrall by my every word on the subject. It's not that I don't think "A-list Gays" (as some people might call them) would be interested in what I talk about. It's just that I genuinely thought they would have some pushback about my stance on a great deal of what goes on in the daily life of someone who is heavily-invested in the stereotypical Gay scene. However, to my surprise, they expressed similar feelings of isolation and sorrow around their own dating experiences with other men and the sense of isolation they felt even when they were surrounded by crowds of men who appeared to adore them. Once again, they confirmed for me something I have always known. Beauty doesn't make Gay dating easier, despite what we are led to believe.

Gay dating is hard all the way around. Good looks can make looking for love just as isolating and lonely as trying to find love,

---

[48] That theory is addressed in *Garbed In Green* and will be expounded upon in this book.

affection, or sex if you don't fit the standard of Gay beauty at the time. One of the guys even said it: "When you're attractive, the Community feels like it owns you. You're public property, and when you turn someone down, it's as if you're stealing from them."

I've always been approachable and friendly when meeting new people, so turning strangers into friends like this was not out of the norm for me. What was out of the norm was how stunningly beautiful these men were. The type of beauty held by their group was rare to see outside of the airbrushed pages of fashion magazines.

As our conversation deepened, I had to keep reminding myself not to go gaga over them. It was so easy for me to slip into romantic thoughts about them. I started to visualize what it might be like to go out on a date with one of them. How he might hold open doors, put his muscular arm around my shoulders and pull me close to his body as we walked. How I might turn my head to catch him caught in a prolonged glance at me, and that seductive, shy smile that he might crack when he recognizes what just happened.

Just as my heart began to beat faster and I realized what was happening to me, one of them asked me to head back to his place with them for a "private party." Immediately all of my fantasies were dashed on the rocks of the reality of Gay "dating,"[49] and I was reminded about just how naive I could be.

I was slightly disappointed by their interest in only the sexual after such a great conversation. I had hoped that our dialogue would have prevented them from agreeing with my philosophy in one breath and proceeding to objectify each other in the next, but I pulled myself together as quickly as possible. There was no reason to ruin an otherwise good afternoon just because the proverbial slipper didn't fit, Cinderella! Instead, I decided to save myself the heartache of feeling used after another purely sexual encounter and go to the local porn shop to pick up my very first dildo so that I could try taking care of myself for a change.

When the idea hit me, it was like the gods hurled a lightning bolt at my head. I was genuinely surprised to find myself

---

[49] Bitter! Party of one!

entertaining the idea, because up until that point in my life, I had never appreciated toys. In fact, I looked down on them. I felt that if I was going to have sex, it was either the real thing or nothing at all; but, dealing with the constant emotional rollercoaster of Gay dating finally got to me, and I broke down and decided to give it a try.

I goose-stepped the three or four blocks over to *Danny's Midnight Confessions* on 13th Street like a disgruntled Ouiser Boudreaux determined to make Drum Eatenton stop shootin' at the birds. I had resolved to buy myself my first dildo and explore this new mindset. I had made a lot of progress on my issues surrounding sex, and I didn't want to slide back into my jaded past just because I was disappointed that another possible Prince Charming had once again revealed himself to be merely another frog.

After all, what really happened? I met some nice guys. We had a great meal and a great conversation, and they expressed their interest in a deeper connection with me. Did it have to be offensive that the deeper connection they wanted was only a matter of inches and not something profoundly deeper? In spite of the spiritual wisdom in that level of tolerance, the size queen in me was unsatisfied.

Despite my newly adopted stance on "self-care" and my vain attempt to quench my silent fury over yet another possible connection being reduced to just sex, I was imminently unprepared for what I found when I arrived in the shop to make my purchase. I felt exposed and vulnerable, like I was that closeted child again exploring Giovanni's Room for the first time.

There was a giant wall of dicks in every shape, size, and color imaginable, and no real way to differentiate between them that would guarantee a good first experience for me. I worried that some were too small and would only frustrate and annoy me; and, I wasn't quite prepared to throw hot dogs down hallways the next time I slept with someone else over a toy. It really was a bit like finding myself in a perverted version of *Goldilocks and the Three Bears*.

I just stood before the wall of dicks dumbfounded, unable to make a decision and a little embarrassed that I was, yet again, in this awkward position in my own sex life. That said, I must have truly been a sight to see, because when I came back to reality and took stock of the world around me, I saw that I had drawn a bit of an audience.

Standing behind me, watching me with a bemused look on his face, was a gorgeous black man. He was built like a bodybuilder; and under any other set of circumstances, I would have been flattered, but I just wasn't in the mood at that point.

"Which one do you like?" he asked as he closed the gap between us.

I don't know why it felt awkward for me to talk with another customer about products in a store we were both frequenting, but my 1950s pearl-clutching house wife was definitely taken aback by his casual familiarity. During my own spiritual practice, I am constantly endeavoring to overcome the Christian-programming that most people in Western Society suffer from around sex. The best way I have found to do that is to constantly remind myself of Sybil Leek's Tenet of Tolerance. It doesn't matter what other people choose to do with their bodies, and it doesn't impact me or my own chosen activities to allow them the freedom to be who they are and express themselves how they feel they need to. Unfortunately, that day, my Tenet of Tolerance suffered a bit.

The man just seemed a bit too familiar for a stranger, and I was offended that he felt entitled to insinuate himself into my personal business. At that moment, I imagined to myself that the vulnerability that I was experiencing face-to-face with this stranger must be exactly how straight men feel when another guy saddles up to the urinals and starts a casual conversation with them while they are busy answering "Nature's call."

I politely brushed him off and tried to continue on with my business, but not getting the hint, or simply not caring to heed it, he persisted.

"I think you should try this one," he said as he picked up an 8" black dildo that was honestly a little "girthier" than I was hoping for.

I raised my one eyebrow in a look that would've had Scarlett O'Hara sit up and take notes on Tara's front porch. I had worked a great deal on perfecting her signature look of disdain during college, and I've never ceased being surprised by how often that practice has come in handy. "Oh really? Why's that?" I said.

"It's the most like mine," he said with what I guess was supposed to be a charming smile. In truth, it came off goofy and not charming at all. Then, as if all that weren't bad enough, he had some supposedly "seductive" things to add about how I could just go for the "real thing" instead and how he'd make me see the face of God and all that.

I know I shouldn't have done it. I know it was mean-spirited and I really should have just accepted the flattery and moved on, but I was a little too annoyed at the liberties he was taking with me, and before I could stop myself, I said, "Seems a little small if you ask me."

He genuinely looked hurt, which I did regret, but I also knew that trying to heal the wound I had inflicted would only make things worse, so I let him leave the store without further interaction. The ironic thing is that I actually did wind up purchasing the dildo that, supposedly, looked the most like his dick. After thinking it through, he was right. It was a very nice size. A little girthier than I had originally intended, but all in all, not too big and not too small. This little Goldilocks went home, hoping it would fit "just right."

When I got back to the house, I found myself in yet another awkward situation. I pulled the dildo out of the brown paper bag the store had wrapped it in and placed it on the coffee table in front of me. I stared at it in its unopened plastic packaging when, suddenly, I realized the damn thing actually intimidated me!

There I was, sitting alone in the living room of my mother's empty house, chastising myself as I became ever more aware that I was actively being terrorized by an inanimate object. I felt foolish. It's not like I was some virgin who had yet to see a naked man. In fact, like most Gay men, my sex life could have, and probably should have, been documented for the public good. Aside from its unquestionable educational value, it's just downright hysterical at times. (But those are stories for another day.)

As I came back to the present moment and actively noticed the dildo on the coffee table again, I conceded that this witch still wasn't emotionally or mentally prepared to go upstairs and "do the Devil's dance" quite yet. I figured some liquid courage would pull me out of this ridiculous hesitation, so I went into the kitchen and poured myself a large glass of wine.

Like the first time I kissed someone else, this first felt earth-shattering. It felt as if my world was never going to be the same again. I remember feeling these same emotions as a child, standing on the boarder of sexual maturity. I worried that my life would never be as innocent again. I didn't want to give up the happy, carefree world I lived in, but I also wanted to know what all the fuss was about regarding sex. Though I was equally torn on that early September night, I was no longer worried about my innocence. I had forsaken that long ago, but I was still worried about something.

After two more equally large glasses of wine, I finally felt brave enough to go upstairs and get down to business. Knowing that the best way out of a fear is often plowing right through it, there was no point in further delaying the inevitable. If I didn't like it, I would just throw the offensive object away and be done with it.

So, I picked up the dildo in its packaging and went upstairs. Then I proceeded to lay down some towels on the bed. I was at my mother's house after all, and I'm nothing if not respectful. Also, if I'm being honest, it delayed the event a moment or two longer without me feeling like I was "wimping out."

When there were no more stalling techniques that I could think of, I opened the toy very slowly and took my clothing off item by item. As I stood there naked before the bed with the glossy black dildo on it, I felt decidedly vulnerable. I remember quivering like I was cold, even though I wasn't. My teeth chattered in my mouth, and I had goosebumps all over my body. It was sort of like my first time all over again.

I had thoughts of shame and guilt, like I was doing something really wrong. "Wrong" is the wrong word. I know I wasn't doing anything immoral, but, in my mind, I felt like an abject failure. I felt like each step I took towards that bed took me one step further away from a goal I had held since childhood: finding one man to love me and cherish me. It was like conceding to finally buy a toy and write physical lovers out of the process was admitting defeat and giving up on the idea of ever being loved.

I sat on the edge of that bed and cried, naked and trembling in the dimly lit privacy of my bedroom. I cried because of the loss of my romantic dream. There might never actually be a Prince

Charming for me, and that realization hurt, but I also cried because I felt pathetic in that moment. Something that comes so naturally to others (a joy surrounding sex and the pleasures it brings them) was so difficult for me. Once again, I felt like that scared little boy who was relegated to the Special Ed class rooms in elementary and middle school because I wasn't learning as fast as the other children, which actually happened to me. I felt like the kid who was bullied and picked on and felt that the whole world was out to get him.

Then I actually found myself laughing through the tears. I laughed because I recognized how foolish I was being. This was just seeking pleasure in myself. *It was giving love to someone who had lacked love for so long.* Putting it in that light made all the difference for me.

I've always been a bit more "like a woman" when it comes to love than the other men I know. I seem to need the emotional connection in a way that few other guys readily admit to. Beyond that, there is nothing I can't overcome for someone I love, like we often talk about mothers doing. Whereas, I would be much more inclined to let you bash me or cause me some kind of perceived harm; however, if you were to go after someone I loved, I would raise the armies of the dead and go to battle like a berserker warrior on steroids. Putting myself into the context of an external other who I could take care of seemed to make all the difference in the world in this situation.

Suddenly, the tears dried up, and I was no longer trembling. I laid down on the bed and picked up the dildo and lube. I took a deep breath and committed to just letting go and having the experience ... whatever it was going to be. To my surprise, it wasn't long before I actually began enjoying myself. The beginning stages, which always seem to require patience, are always tiresome to me. That fumbling negotiation of two clunky bodies whenever one takes a new lover always bores me to tears, so why should it be any different in sex with myself. Admittedly, patience is not one of my virtues. It wasn't long before the pleasure took over and I forgot my boredom.

The next time I looked at the clock, three hours had gone by, and I still hadn't sought release. That was unheard of for me. I don't normally like sex to last any longer than it "has to" to get the job done. The fact that I lost track of that much time and actually enjoyed myself was a genuine shock.

It was now nearly two o'clock in the morning, and I wanted to get to bed. So, even though I could have probably gone another hour or two, I took the first opportunity to release for practical reasons. After cleaning up, I rolled over and drifted off to sleep, but it wasn't until the next day that I realized how profoundly that event actually impacted me.

This was the first time since my failed relationship with Josh that I truly took care of myself sexually. I'm not sure why this sexual experience was different than all the others in-between. Maybe I was struggling with some leftover damage from the times that I was raped, which wouldn't allow me to let go with another person. I was willing to consider that. I hated it because it seemed so broken and weak, but I had to concede that it was possible. However, I'm also profoundly willful. I've always had an iron will, so I couldn't rule out the possibility of this being my own, weird form of silent protest against an overarching Gay Culture, which promotes emotional negligence with each other. I truly resented the idea that, in the past, men have refused to invest in me emotionally before they had the chance to have sex with me. Someone actually told me that dating is a bit like buying a car. Nobody is going to sign on the dotted line until they take the car out for a spin. I may not have had the option to withhold the keys from them, but I could certainly prevent them from revving my engine! Given that particular stance, I also couldn't rule out spite as a viable contender to answer the question. Whatever the real reason is that I had never enjoyed sex with someone else as much as I did with that inanimate object, I can't say. I started to compare that one sexual experience to all the other past experiences with previous lovers or hook ups, and I began to wonder why it had taken me so long to ditch the other men entirely and finally take this solo step on the path to my own personal healing.

6 POLARITY & GAY DATING

The Law of Polarity and the Principle of Gender are distinct. Though they are often conflated or confused by otherwise adept witches, I, personally, have not found them to be the same. The Law of Polarity embodies the principle that all manifested things have two sides, aspects, or poles that are only separated by shades of degrees between the two extremes. Hot and Cold, Good and Bad, Dark and Light—there is no definitive point where one boundary stands firm against the other. Pairs of opposites, which hold a unification at their core, like the Yin-Yang symbol also embody this principal. "Everything is and isn't at the same time." Polarity helps us overcome paradox. The Principle of Gender, on the other hand, is where the Masculine and Feminine forces actually come into question. It states that Masculine and Feminine Principles are at work on every plane of existence. On the Physical Plane they manifest as sex. On the higher planes, this Principle takes on higher forms according to the nature of the plane in question. No creation (physical, mental, or spiritual) can exist without the Principle of Gender. It is also worth mentioning here that *The Kybalion*, which was first published in 1908, states outright Gender and biological sex are not the same.

In my opinion, this is where some witches get it wrong. An initiation is viewed to be a re-birth of sorts for a witch—a primal act of creation. As we just saw, there can be no creation without applying the Principle of Gender. That does not, however, necessarily mean an exclusive heterosexual pairing is necessary to receive initiation.

Biological sex is only the manifestation of the Principle of Gender on the Physical Plane. However, as modern psychology has pointed out for over a century, men often have an internal Feminine principle to their minds and women often have an internal Masculine quality. As I hope this book will make plain, the power of the witch is the power of thought. Therefore, the mental genders of the initiate and initiator must necessarily be taken into account when initiating a witch. Whether or not the biological sex is ALSO a factor is obviously up to each individual coven.

While more conservative covens undoubtedly have the best intentions, I have seen this particular discrepancy cause significant harm to Gay men, Lesbians, and Transgender people in the near past. Unfortunately, I have also seen this harm Wicca as a religion. The hatred and vehemence that many offended LGBTQIA people and our allies publicly spew at Wicca as they turn away from the religion over this piece of heteronormativity is a direct result of the harm, which I am talking about. In truth, I can't blame them for their indignation.

I remember a specific event from a few years back when I started studying the Male Mysteries. This was before I had established Gala Witchcraft as a tradition. I had just earned my third degree in the coven where I entered the priesthood, and I was very proud of myself and of Wicca in general. I loved (and still do love) this religion. I loved that it was so accepting, especially of Queer people. I was tired of seeing mainstream religion tear us down, and I was so pleased that Wicca didn't do that … at least as far as I knew.

Then I met a British boy named Kyle online. We talked a bit about the Craft and how he couldn't find a coven in England, which surprised me greatly. Everything I had heard up to that point made England sound like the heart and soul of witchcraft.

As I pressed Kyle for further details, it turned out that there were, indeed, plenty of covens near him. He just couldn't find one that would allow him to circle with them as a Gay man. If he wanted to initiate into their circles, he would have to be willing to leave his homosexuality out of their rituals and partner with a woman in a heterosexual working pair relationship within the coven.

Apparently, the covens he approached adamantly professed their support of LGBTQIA rights, but they insisted that even though an individual man could be Gay, the High Priest as a functionary role never could. The function of the High Priest in their mind was necessarily heterosexual, and if Kyle wasn't willing to leave his sexuality out of circle, they would have to agree to disagree, and he would have to find another coven or go it alone.

When I heard that, it upset me. Personally, I think that Queer people have had to compromise who we are for far too long, and I do not believe that we should continue to do so in this day and age. I certainly don't think that we should deny our sexuality in something as important and as personal as our religion or spirituality, especially not when our religion claims to be a "nature" religion that embraces Matriarchy, revels in all forms of sexuality, and publicly professes to support LGBTQIA people.

The fact that LGBTQIA people still seek out witchcraft but wrongly believe that Wicca is obsolete or in some other way deficient because of this dispute is a shame. As I said in *Garbed In Green*, Wicca might accurately be considered the modern incarnation of the Temple Priesthood for the Ancient Wisdom Religion, whereas witchcraft is more akin to common folk magical practices. These two manifestations of the Magical Art are intimately tied together as one spirituality with various expressions of their basic tenets. Seeing these two paths as divergent and distinct only clouds the issue and creates unnecessary divisions.

The truth is that Wicca as an overarching religion, independent of any one coven or Tradition, is very accepting of LGBTQIA people. Not only does it accept us, it revels in our existence. It recognizes our power and the gifts that we bring to the table.[50] I feel that it would be an equal tragedy for Wicca to lose out on the unique flavor of LGBTQIA priests and priestesses and for the LGBTQIA Community to lose out on the healing potential and spiritual enrichment that Wicca has to offer. This is one of the reasons that I created Gala Witchcraft, and it is one of the reasons I am so firm in my desire to help Transgender people to reclaim their own Mystery Tradition to uplift them as well. While I support women and Lesbians, I don't have anything to offer them in this regard, because Lesbians already have several options for exploring the Female Mysteries in an affirming way.

It is so easy to cast stones at some witches regarding their practice of cross-gender initiations. In fact, I have heard many self-identified Gay male witches make a point of drawing their battle lines on this issue of Polarity and Gender alone. However,

---

[50] For a better understanding of how, refer to *Garbed In Green*. I go into greater detail on this subject in that book.

that's not entirely fair. The truth is that even Gay men struggle with confusing these two principles by merging physical sex and gender in our own dating lives. Lacking a deeper understanding of the occult principles at work in our relationships with each other, we find ourselves isolated and alone far more often than we have to be. If we grapple with these concepts within our own community in 2019, how can we be upset that the more traditional covens struggle with the same issues? Some of these covens have been around for the better of a century and have proof that their practices work.

Too often, especially on the hookup apps, you find men who can "pass" for Straight requiring their partners to be just as "straight-acting" as they are. They fetishize masculinity and actively look down on anyone who is "too Gay." They spout bigotry and hate like "If I wanted to be with a woman, I'd be straight" and justify it as preference. In addition to being misogynistic and demeaning to both women and Gay men, this is a recipe for disaster for that poor soul. At its core, this "preference" perpetuates the idea that being either feminine or Gay is somehow shameful. However, it is these same "Straight acting" Gay men who are the most hurt by this unfortunate belief. It sets up their relationships with each other for failure and prevents them from finding a lasting and loving union with someone who might be a better fit for them.

The reason that actual Straight men can have these "bromances" with each other, which look so sexually appealing to some Gay men, is precisely because the Straight men involved are not looking for anything more than being friends, despite how Gay men sexualize their connection from the outside looking in. If the bromance is actually sexual between the two men involved, I would argue that they are no longer purely Straight. They may be Bisexual and choose to identify as "primarily Straight," but they cease actually being completely Straight the moment they routinely seek sexual satisfaction from another man or fetishize his body. Admittedly, this piece about "Straight" guys losing their "Straight status" upon having regular sexual interactions with each other may also be my own prejudice. I'm willing to concede that. That said, the simple fact remains: actual Straight men are not trying to build a long-term romantic or loving relationship with each other while also donning the *Straight* label. Necessarily, their sexual and romantic interests reside with women if they are actually *Straight*.

Despite how they interact with each other, when Straight men want to build a romantic life with a woman, they generally look for a mate who expresses some opposite that will enhance their lives. She's negative, cold, creative, etc. He's positive, hot, rational, etc. They function off Polarity, which is one reason that their relationships work so well when they actually do work. They do not confuse their momentary satisfaction with their long-term goals. Gay men, viewing Straight male relationships from the outside, fail to take that unspoken discernment into account when fetishizing the "bonds of brotherhood" between actual Straight men or between "Straight acting" Bisexual men.

For Gay men who fetishize these pack-like relationships, the interactions are anything but platonic. Seeking to avoid intimacy with effeminate men, these "Straight-acting" Gay men fool themselves into thinking that the intimacy which they feel for their friend could actually work out as a real bona fide long-term or committed partnership. It's sad really, because this delusion will ultimately leave them alone and unhappy.

The problem is that when Gay men fetishize Masculinity in our prospective partners, we lose balance. Remember, all acts of creation require the pairing of the Masculine and Feminine Genders. By only focusing on the Masculine and by insisting that our partners "be real men" or ridiculing them for having Feminine qualities, we fail to allow ourselves the opportunity to create the energetic connection needed to birth a solid and lasting relationship.

That is not to say that you can't seek Masculinity in a partner. If you happen to be a Gay man with a more Feminine disposition (like the stereotypical Twink), it is actually advisable that you prioritize a Masculine nature in your romantic partner. If, on the other hand, you happen to be more Masculine in your own self-expression, you need to be more discerning in this regard. If you are sexually turned on by the typical, red-blooded, American Male depictions of masculinity, that's okay. The men who fit the bill would make excellent friends with benefits for you. You can still have sex with men who express this quality. Just don't make the tragic mistake of trying to build a life with them as your romantic partner.

A simple elementary school science experiment teaches us this lesson plainly. Hold the North poles of two magnets together and they will repel each other. However, face one magnet's South pole towards the North pole of the other, and the two collide with an undeniable force. The same is true in attraction regarding people. In *The Secret Doctrine*, H. P. Blavatsky reveals the same truth from a metaphysical perspective when talking about Fohat and his role within esoteric cosmologies. According to Blavatsky, "This, of course, relates, as anyone can see, to electricity generated by friction and to the law involving attraction between two objects of unlike, and repulsion between those of like polarity."[51]

This ancient Hermetic wisdom is actually the key to helping Gay men overcome a major hurdle in finding the love that we desire with each other. Necessarily, all the bodies present in a Gay male relationship will be of the male sex. As I said in *Garbed In Green* while talking about the magical dynamo, we cannot get away from the fact that, despite our balanced spiritual energies and the attending predisposition to magic that this balance provides us, our male bodies do tip the scale in favor of the electric polarity. If you remember, the electric polarity has a tendency to project outward, to repel, which is one of the metaphysical reasons why Gay male relationships are so stereotypically short-lived.[52]

Rather than not being "man enough," as our enemies claim, Gay men are over-saturated with male energies. The electric nature of this over-saturation actually keeps us apart, and it must be accounted for if we are going to overcome this particular hurdle to our unions. The Hermetic Law of Polarity and the Principle of Gender help wise Gay male witches compensate for this imbalance.

We can do nothing about the male bodies involved. They are

---

[51] Blavatsky, H. P. The Secret Doctrine I. The Theosophical Publishing Company, Limited, 1888, 145.

[52] I talk about the properties of the magnetic and electric polarities and their effects on Gay male relationships in Garbed In Green. If you would like to trace my research on this subject, I would recommend that you read the work of Gavin and Yvonne Frost and Franz Bardon's Initiation Into Hermetics.

part and parcel of the package. However, we can regulate the mental genders of the partners in question.

The idea of Mental Gender is an ancient Hermetic doctrine, which has found its way into some schools of modern Psychology, albeit in very modified forms. Though the various schools of thought differ slightly, the basic premise is this: The mind is dual in nature. For Hermeticism, the two principles of Mind belong to the Masculine and the Feminine. The Masculine Principle of Mind corresponds to the active, conscious, and voluntary, while the Feminine Principle of Mind corresponds to the passive, subconscious, and involuntary.[53]

Psychology tends to talk about these in various ways, depending on the school of thought the psychologist follows, but the most common depiction is right and left brain, creative and rational. Regardless of the theory, the point is the same: the mental sphere is the primary place where Gay men can offset the electric polarity of their physical bodies, which keeps their relationships from being more long-lasting.

This leads us to something that I believe is a huge problem within the Gay Community: our friendships and romantic relationships are being pulled from the same pool. It is often difficult, if not impossible, to tell the difference between a hookup, a potential friend, and someone who is primed to be quality dating material at first, second, or even third glance. Straight society has built in systems to help them navigate this social hurdle. "Straight" guys may fetishize each other, as we've discussed, but the boundaries of their relationships with each other are ready-made. They know that no matter what their momentary connection is, no matter how similar they are and how much those similarities enhance their friendships, they are going

---

[53] A deeper explanation of the Hermetic theory on Mental Gender is unnecessary and will only serve to confuse readers who have not studied the full system with distinctions between "the I" and "the Me" and various other metaphysical concepts. The basic gist is that there are two minds and that they have a gender. Should you wish to study this further before embarking on your own exploration of Mental Gender, begin with The Kybalion. If, however, you are happy with my cursory overview and the general gist will suffice to get you to the next step in this process, carry on.

to settle down with a woman. As for Straight dating, it too has built-in rules, parameters, and obligations that are universally recognized. Gay men, necessarily, don't have that. Instead, we revel in our lack of those structures, rules, and parameters. Like a vine climbing up a trellis, the Gay Community needs some structure or it will get trampled underfoot. We need to come to some point of balance between the confining heteronormative rules that we ditched when we blew the hinges off our closet doors and the free-for-all that our current interactions with each other have degraded into.

Ultimately, the primary confusion in Gay dating stems from the fact that our community is built up almost exclusively around finding sex. It shouldn't be. There is so much more to actual Gay life than the sex that we have with other men. Unfortunately, those other components take a back seat (if not get jettisoned from the car entirely) to the flashier, sexualized veneer, which is draped over the Gay Community.

When a Jewish person prizes his culture, he talks about the wisdom and learning of the rabbis, the beauty and mystery of the Kabbalah, or the strength of character of his people. He talks about the travesty of the Holocaust or the struggles that Jewish people have had to endure throughout history. When an Italian prizes his culture, he talks about the good food, the great works of art, and the passion of his people. The same is true for nearly every other culture or racial group on earth today. They prioritize great achievements and contributions, which their people have made to society.

Not so with Gay men!

Gay culture actually exists, just like Jewish or Italian culture. In literature alone, we have so many people to look up to and be proud of. The poetry of Lord Byron is truly a work of art. Oscar Wilde was as well-known as a dandy as he was a poet, and in both cases, he is someone worthy of respect. His work brought Gay love out of the dark ages, and his staunch refusal to deny who he was and be punished for it shows an internal strength comparable to the physical strength of Hercules or any other mythic god. Walt Whitman's *Fierce Wrestler* is a poem so homoerotic that it should hold us all in awe that he succeeded at getting it out to the general public in 1847. James Baldwin's *Giovanni's Room* is a classic on par with anything written by Hemingway, Fitzgerald, or Steinbeck, and it deserves to be appreciated by the world for its elegant beauty. Allan Ginsberg wrote a poem about Gay love in 1981 called *Old Love Story*. In my opinion every Gay man should read it.

Gay men are so much more than what we currently present ourselves to be. The Gay Community could and should have real pride for what we have brought into the world, but instead, we focus on flashing our dicks in an endless parade of Dionysian ecstasy. We forget that Apollo was also a Gay god and that his contributions to our mental and spiritual lives are equally worthy of praise.

Once we get away from the idea that the Gay Community and Gay life in general has to be built up around sex or finding the next boyfriend, we can begin to see things more clearly. Dating becomes part of what we do, not who we are, and, in making that simple mental shift, it becomes easier. Granted, the masculine ideals that turn us all on so much are alluring, but if you fit that masculine ideal yourself and you want to achieve a lasting and loving union (instead of just sex), it would be better to remember that "birds of a feather flock together, but opposites attract."

Mental Mapping

Should you wish to take advantage of this occult theory, turn your attention inward and take stock of your own mental character. Use whatever system you want. If you subscribe to one of the many modern psychological theories on this subject, use it. Personally, as a former philosophy major, I love Nietzsche's concept of the Apollonian and the Dionysian, with the Apollonian standing in for the Male and the Dionysian being more Feminine in nature. Whatever system you use, make sure to honor it fully and apply it faithfully.

Make three lists. The first should be labeled *Masculine Mind*. The second should be labeled *Feminine Mind*. The third should be labeled *Lover*.

1. Under Masculine Mind, list as many masculine mind traits as you can think of or find (i.e., analytical, intellectual, objective, mathematical, etc.).

2. Under Feminine Mind, list as many feminine mind traits as you can think of or find (i.e., creative, emotional, subjective,

artistic, etc.)

3. Go through both lists and highlight each of the characteristics that you believe you possess.

4. After highlighting the Masculine Mind and Feminine Mind lists, write the corresponding polar opposite traits on your Lover list.

Be thorough and exacting. Work on your lists for as long as you need to in order to be certain that you have scoured every possible nook and cranny of your own mind.

Put the lists away for a week. Turn your mind to other thoughts. Then when you come back, take stock.

Ask yourself: "Do I like the mental picture of my Lover?" Spend some time daydreaming about what it might be like to be in a relationship with someone who expressed those particular qualities. If any quality on that Lover list upsets you or makes you think that you couldn't be with someone who expressed it, you can modify your own mind and eliminate the quality that corresponds to the offending item. This book has practices that will help you with this process.

7 DESIRE: WANTING IT BAD ENOUGH

All magic begins with desire. Magical success, however, begins after you learn to utilize desire effectively. That requires us to control our reactions to the people and things, which excite our emotions. Only by fully understanding the true nature of desire and learning how to use its vast power correctly will you be able to achieve the success that you want in love.

Should you wish to become proficient in the Witch's Art, it is not merely enough to eliminate all desire, like the Buddhists are said to do. Instead, you must learn to utilize it. Eliminating all desire is certainly a wonderful aim if your goal is spiritual evolution. On this the Buddhist and the witch agree, but the spirit's course through reincarnation is not what we are discussing in this book. Our current goal revolves around helping Gay male witches find the love they want.

Desire can be a wonderful tool to help you do just that. It can overcome obstacles that nothing else can. Unfortunately, when misused, it can also derail your progress towards your goals, as far too many Gay men will attest. So, if you are going to attempt to harness Desire for your witchy purposes, it would be wise to understand its strengths and limitations.

However, Desire cannot be fully understood without also understanding the full metaphysical composition of the mind or soul. That desire originates in the mind might seem novel or even wrong to some readers, but it is essential that we acknowledge this piece of the puzzle. In fact, Desire is part of one of three overarching faculties that make up the sum total of the mind's powers: Feeling (to which Desire belongs), Thinking, and Willing.

Most people have no problem associating Thinking and Willing with the mind, but we tend to divorce Feeling from the mental sphere entirely. Instead, we talk about Feeling as if it were a bodily sensation (like the sense of touch or a gut feeling) or we mysteriously connect it with some other part of our being (like the metaphorical heart). Rarely do people consider that Feeling is actually of the same ilk as Thinking or that it might be happening in the same region of the mind as Willing.

According to W. W. Atkinson in his book *Desire Power or Your Energizing Forces*, Feeling is just "the agreeable or disagreeable phase of a mental state."[54] As such, it is intimately tied to Thinking and Willing in a very concrete way. Intellect, the most prized asset of our Thinking capacity in the Western World, is influenced, swayed, directed, and sometimes entirely controlled by the faculty of Feeling through the emotions it generates. How often do orators, scientists, lawyers, and other supposedly "rational" professionals argue for or attempt to prove a theory that justifies their biases instead of gazing upon their circumstances through the cold light of reason alone? Whereas the intellect is only partially controlled by the emotions, the Will has every one of its motives instigated by Emotion.

Not only is Feeling associated with the mind, it actually claims supremacy within the psychic domain. Feeling exists wholly by itself, irreducible by any external force. Indeed, it is the foundation upon which the other two modes of mental operation are constructed. Feeling cannot be derived from either of the other two mental faculties. It is not a mode or a function of the Intellect nor of the Thinking power in general, and though emotions and desires can be influenced by the person's Will,[55] he still has to desire to exercise his Will upon those emotions before any change can be made.

Up until now, I have been using the words *Feeling*, *Emotion*, and *Desire* as interchangeable. However, they do have differences, and it is essential that we address those differences before we move on to applying this wisdom. We have already discussed Feeling as "the agreeable or disagreeable phase of a mental state." Atkinson defines Emotion as "a complex form of Feeling, into which is

---

[54] Atkinson, W. W. and Edward E. Beals. *Desire Power or Your Energizing Forces*. Robert Collier Book Corp, 1975, 6.

[55] Atkinson and Beals refer to this exact scenario as "the Will to Will."

blended the element of the representative idea of memory or imagination."[56]

Emotion, then, owes its existence, in part, to the Thinking faculty, which is just more proof positive that Feeling belongs to the realm of the mind. If Feeling weren't mental, how else would it be able to blend with Thinking into Emotion? Establishing the mental credentials for Feeling and Emotion, Atkinson goes on to tell us that "Desire is the strong urge or pressure of Emotion toward an idea or object which promises emotional satisfaction and content; or away from an idea or object which threatens emotional dissatisfaction or discontent."[57]

While Desire may be viewed as the highest wave of the waters of Feeling and Emotion, there are smaller waves of emotion, which crest above these deep waters. Less complex than Desire, Affection is defined as: "An emotional drawing of the mind toward any person or thing, which does not necessarily depart even when that person or thing is absent."[58] Atkinson tells us that Affection is composed of two elements: the Emotional Feeling and the tendency to be attracted toward (or repelled from[59]) the object arousing the emotional feeling. In its active state, Affection might present as Passion. In this model, Passion is merely the most intense form of Affection.

This distinction between Affection, Passion, and Desire is the key to successfully raising energy for magical purposes. We tend to talk about Passion and Desire as if they are the same thing, but

---

[56] Atkinson, W. W. and Edward E. Beals. *Desire Power or Your Energizing Forces. Robert Collier Book Corp, 1975, 6.*

[57] Atkinson, W. W. and Edward E. Beals. *Desire Power or Your Energizing Forces. Robert Collier Book Corp, 1975, 6-7.*

[58] Atkinson, W. W. and Edward E. Beals. *Desire Power or Your Energizing Forces. Robert Collier Book Corp, 1975, 8.*

[59] When Affection is repelled from something, it is because it is attracted to its opposite. The force of Attraction is actually magnetic. It attracts and is attracted to an object. When it moves away from another object, it is because the magnetic pull of that object's opposite draws it away, not because Affection, itself, produces its own electric force.

they are not. Passion is a weaker emotion than Desire, weaker in the sense that it is less intense and doesn't generate as much power. **It is important that we put Desire and Passion in their correct order from the outset or it will be very difficult (if not impossible) to achieve magical success.**

Just as Emotion, as a whole, shares a piece of both Feeling and Thinking, Desire may be said to share a piece of all three mental powers. It has the elements of Feeling and Thinking that all other emotional states have, but it may also be considered the transition into the Will. "Emotion rising to Desire, tends to become transformed into Will,"[60] according to Atkinson.

The true potential of our Feeling faculty is profound. It is not some triviality that can be tossed about carelessly. Yet so many people today do just that, pitching fits and engaging in pointless outbursts. More than just overindulging in this facet of themselves, they are all so very attached to their emotions. Some of them even use emotions to define who they are. The same can be said for our thoughts. Many people are attached to the things they think, as if their ideas were a part of them. The older occult writers talked about thoughts as if they were independent things floating around in a room or a space that influenced us whenever we came in contact with them, and they were right to do so.

If you did the elemental servitor exercise earlier in this book, you already have some personal experience with this concept. Thoughts and ideas are, in fact, entities. They exist independently of man. They can be set into motion, however, by the Will. You did exactly that when you created your elemental servitor to help you get ready to find a partner.

To see further proof of the validity in the old occult philosophy, just consider a time when you had an original thought that you failed to act on. Many of those thoughts simply disappeared back into the ether from whence they came, never to be dealt with again. Some ignored thoughts, however, resurfaced in your life as the expression of someone else's genius.

Would-be inventors talk about this concept all the time. They

---

[60] Atkinson, W. W. and Edward E. Beals. *Desire Power or Your Energizing Forces.* Robert Collier Book Corp, 1975, 20.

get an idea for an invention. They write it off as foolish, impractical, or in some other way impossible, and then a few years later, they see the product of their exact idea for sale on the shelves at some store.

This very thing happened to me as a child. Every time we had a formal affair to go to, I would pitch the most ungodly fit because of the dress clothes that were available for me to wear. I still hate what qualifies for men's fashion in formal wear, for the record. The attire they make men wear is atrocious. Just look at any wedding party. The women are all so beautiful and the men are little more than drones that can't be told apart. Looking at Nature and how she so wisely endowed the peacock with his beautiful plumage or the robin with his red breast to draw the attention of predators away from their mates, the human desire to dull men's colors seems unnatural to me.

I remember one time, I came upstairs in a button-down shirt that literally looked like a parachute on me. It was 10 sizes too big for my body, and I was so annoyed that my sisters got to look glamourous in their dresses, which showed off all the best parts of their bodies. Meanwhile, I had to settle for what amounted to a drab, monochromatic discarded circus tent. I ripped the Barnum and Bailey's reject off of my torso and threw it on the ground, refusing to go to any more formal events until I could find something that allowed me to accentuate my body rather than hide it from the world.

"Why," I argued, "should a man's muscular back be hidden from the world when a woman can wear a backless dress?"

Furthermore, why shouldn't a man be able to show off his powerful thighs if a woman can walk around with her legs exposed for all the world to see? Truth be told, I could probably make this argument point for point about any body part that formal attire allows women to accentuate but sees fit to hide on men.

Needless-to-say, my mom was nonplussed back then, and her attitude hasn't improved much on this topic over the years. She just calls me "Scarlett" and rolls her eyes, and we agree to move on. Whenever I have gotten too prissy or "uppity" for my mother's taste, she likened me to Scarlett O'Hara from *Gone With The Wind* in a vain attempt to shame me into proper or respectable behavior. Well, the jokes on her. I like the association. Scarlett was strong and resourceful, and, more to the point, she got to wear formal attire that actually made her look good. So, fiddle dee dee, Linda!

Anyway, I digress. A few years later, Banana Republic came out with the first fitted button-down shirt. It was a bitter-sweet victory for me. I was thrilled that I finally had something I could wear to formal events that didn't make me feel like the Blob. It wasn't perfect. It still hid all the best parts of a man's body, in my opinion, but it was better than nothing. That said, I was also a little cranky that I didn't get the credit for coming up with the idea first. I could've made a mint!

Our sense of Feeling operates exactly the same way as our thoughts do. Though we talk about emotions as if we generate them, they are not necessarily our own. The things we feel do not always belong to us in the same way that our right hand does. To see that this is true, all one has to do is look at a mob that has been incited to riot. The emotion which propels that mob is infectious, and everyone who wanders blindly across its path runs the risk of being swept away in the "excitement." The same thing happens at concerts and sporting events.

The term *Emotional* has become synonymous with "drama" and the kind of low-class outburst one might see on *Keeping Up with the Kardashians*, *The Bachelor*, *Honey Boo Boo*, *Celebrity Big Brother*, or any of the other countless television shows that aid in the devolution of the human species. That is truly unfortunate, because Emotion and Feeling instills existence with meaning. Some of the very best aspects of life stem from this faculty.

Whether a particular spiritual path enriches one's life or leaves the person feeling flat is due almost exclusively to Emotion. As witches, we experienced this truth the first time we stepped into our circles. The experience was so moving and emotional that it felt like "coming home" to many of us. The emotions and the Feeling faculty in general help us to find our place in this world. Without the emotional pull on the heart, many a witch would never have set foot on this Crooked Path we all love so much.[61]

"Remove Emotion from human life, and you will have taken away the source of its greatest beauties and charm."[62] Affection, love, friendship—none of these things can exist without Emotion. Ambition, progress, indeed achievement of any kind at all owe a debt to Emotion.

The witch's path is one of balance. Necessarily then, we must apply our Tenet of Balance to the regulation of Emotion as well as anything else. The truth is that we witches seek to recognize the power inherent in our emotions and to use them appropriately without letting them run roughshod over our lives.

Yes, Emotion is the source of some of the richest and most noble elements of life, but that is exactly why it must not be contaminated by adolescent and neurotic behavior, like my hissy fit over the circus tent my mother tried to force on me. There is a very practical side to Emotion and Feeling, and we lose out on tapping into that resource when we begin to devalue the emotions. Therefore, a wise witch balances his Intellect, Emotion, and Will to avoid this loss of personal power.

As the beginning stages of the Will, Desire can be deployed to get us exactly what we want. Left unattended though, it can also pull us far off course. In order to take advantage of its positive benefits, all we need to do is learn how to harness it correctly and not waste its immense power on extraneous things that drain us or pull us in countless directions at once.

Desire is not frivolous or shallow, as so many people seem to think of it today. It has nothing to do with buying the next designer outfit, the most luxurious car, or even how someone else

---

[61] For the record, this is true of every religious path. The Christian undoubtedly feels the same way. In fact, I have spoken with many Catholics in my own life who "feel uplifted" by the Catholic Mass, especially around the Christmas season. That their faith calls to them and not me is due to this quality of Feeling in the mind, and I, for one, am so grateful that I feel the pull of this path and not that one.

[62] Atkinson, W. W. and Edward E. Beals. *Desire Power or Your Energizing Forces.* Robert Collier Book Corp, 1975, 12.

makes you feel. Those are Passions.

Rather, Desire is essential to life. It is an internal need for some necessary thing, like a drowning man needs air or a starving man needs nourishment. Desire is the one mental element present universally in all living things.[63] It manifests in three general ways in every living thing from the smallest plant to a human being: (1) the desire to preserve the physical body, (2) satiating the hunger response, and (3) satisfying the procreative drive.

The "desire to preserve the physical body," which Atkinson labels as Desire's first manifestation, has been referred to by many other names: the survival instinct, the will to live, and self-preservation, just to name a few. It is an instinctive drive that cannot be ignored or reasoned past. Even the most pessimistic individual will fight for his very survival as he laments life's emptiness. This basic instinct is the well-spring from which most other desires are derived.

It is this level of intensity that witches are talking about when we talk about Desire in magic. If your "want" or "want to" doesn't reach this level of intensity, it is only a Passion and your chances of success are greatly diminished. This is especially true if you are competing against someone else who is able to generate this level of Desire at a moment's notice. It is not enough to merely want something, like you do with a Passion; you must need it like the rabbit needs to outrun the fox or the ivy vine needs to creep towards the sunlight.

The Will to Live implants a strong and insistent urge in each creature to seek out nourishment. Many secondary desires stem from this craving. To see what I mean, all you have to do is look at a culture experiencing famine. No matter how civilized or advanced a society is, the moment food sources become scarce, all that's society's refinement and culture go out the window. When that happens, humanity reverts back to its hunter-gatherer days with all the concerns of that era in full force.

The desire to reproduce is elemental. The mating instinct cannot be ignored, and it is the root cause of our desire for sexual

---

[63] Atkinson, W. W. and Edward E. Beals. *Desire Power or Your Energizing Forces.* Robert Collier Book Corp, 1975, 42.

fulfillment. This is true regardless of whether we're talking about sexual interactions that produce physical offspring or not—whether we're talking about homosexual or heterosexual pairings. In all people, the procreative drive expresses itself along two general lines: (1) the love of mates and (2) the care and protection of the offspring.[64]

Unlike the other two foundational Desires mentioned so far, the procreative drive is not just concerned with the preservation of the individual's life. Rather, it is forcibly and intensely concerned with the propagation of the species as a whole. Contrary to the concern for individual life, this particular expression of Desire is so strong that the individual may sometimes willingly sacrifice himself in order to copulate. This level of self-sacrifice can often be seen within the animal kingdom during mating season. Dame Nature rightly made this Desire to supersede all the others, for without the urge to pass on the "Flame of Life," as Atkinson calls it, life on Earth would wane uncontrollably.

When considered in this light, it becomes more understandable why we single Gay men occupy so much of our time with the search for sex or love. Once again, it makes no difference that our sexual release together does not produce biological offspring. The Desire to reproduce our genes is still the driving force behind the urge that compels us to seek each other out. Companionship is a foundational and basic human need, just like food, shelter, and safety. Without an appropriate outlet for the procreative drive to express itself, quality of life is greatly diminished.

My single biggest frustration when writing this chapter has been trying to answer one simple question. Why does society trivialize and ridicule fixation in the search for love when we prize

---

[64] Though some Gay men have chosen to have children, either by adopting them or through scientific intervention, I am going to choose to leave this topic alone in this book. Strictly speaking, in a completely natural state, Gay sex does not reproduce on the material plane, so it is irrelevant to talk further about this topic in a magical book designed to help Gay men navigate their desire for love and union. Even if physical reproduction were a natural part of the Gay male experience, it still wouldn't be germane to the topic of this book, as this book deals with the process of getting to that point, not that point or beyond.

an equally persistent determination regarding the attainment of other basic human needs? When someone is homeless and doggedly puts in the work to secure housing for himself, we hold him up as an example to be followed. We often cheer that "He pulled himself up by his bootstraps!" When someone spends every waking moment concerned with "putting food on the table" for his family, we glorify him as a *good provider*. When a single person puts an equal amount of attention into finding a mate, however, we call him "obsessed," "broken," or "pathetic."

I believe the reason for this societal disdain is twofold. First, Western Culture disdains sex, especially blatant or unabashed demonstrations of sex. The single person who "obsesses" about dating or laments his single status too loudly or too often reminds us that our own version of "transcendent" love has nothing more than base sexual lust at its root. Somehow this realization "cheapens" the very concept of "loving union" and the construct of the nuclear family in the collective opinion. Second, people generally appreciate proficiency. It's not enough to work hard. It must be the right kind of hard work in order to be laudable. A homeless man who begs on the street corner for his supper is not praised as a role model, no matter how effective he is at his task; and nobody appreciates Rapunzel's proficiency at "maintaining her hair" when they watch *Into the Woods*.

Regarding the first reason, the undisguised sexualization of the Gay Community is a mark against us. Though it's unfortunate that this judgmental public opinion holds so much sway, it is one of the reasons why Gay men lack support in issues surrounding our relationships. Personally, I believe that this lack of support is one of the greatest factors contributing to why so many Gay men suffer issues of isolation and loneliness, especially in later life. Most people in the West simply do not want to be confronted by sex and sexuality, and it is easier to write others off than to address our own fears around these uncomfortable topics.

Atkinson highlights the very perspective I'm talking about when he says, "In the case of primitive man, the mating instinct is little more than the sex instinct of the lower animals; the mating was for but a brief period, and mates were changed with the seasons. But, as man ascended the scale, the mating instinct took on a higher, more complex, and more permanent form. There gradually dawned upon the race-consciousness the idea of Home and Family—of a more permanent union."[65] While I, as a witch, personally agree with the spirit of Atkinson's statement, his verbiage does indicate a commonly-held disdain for the more carnal aspects of the sex drive.

I have always felt that if one wanted to be an effective witch, then he must be willing to allow his higher self to guide his course, not his ego and certainly not his base, unfiltered sex drive. Just because we have an urge, doesn't mean that we have to exercise it. As with the emotions, the Tenet of Balance calls for us to recognize the sex drive in its proper place, not to glorify it and not to demean it. Sex is a tool to be used to good effect, but it should never be our master.

As for the second reason for society's disdain of the single man's plight, the truth is that most single people, especially single Gay men, are not approaching being single in a way that is effective at bringing about the result they desire. This ineptitude is offensive to a large portion of society. It's offensive in the same way that watching a terrible acting performance on TV or seeing someone embarrass himself publicly without recognizing his blunder is offensive. It just hurts the onlooker too much to watch it. Unlike fulfilling the other basic human needs, the desire for a mate is not something one can pursue with tenacity. Rather, as trite as this sounds and as much as I hate telling you (precisely because it is trite), the solution lies with finding love within oneself first. Once someone attains this level of self-sufficiency, a loving mate is more readily available.

If you are going to pursue the goal of finding a relationship with the ardent passion that most single Gay men invest in this search, it would be far better to engage in an active and consistent practice of self-improvement than to constantly seek out partners on the hookup apps, on dating websites, or in the Gay bars. I know that's not a popular answer to this conundrum. It is, however, an effective one.

Instead of wasting time in those futile endeavors, take up a

---

[65] Atkinson, W. W. and Edward E. Beals. *Desire Power or Your Energizing Forces.* Robert Collier Book Corp, 1975, 56-57.

general practice of meditation and learn to quiet your mind. An unsettled mind is the biggest impediment to your success in this venture. Get involved in hobbies and experiences that make your soul sing. Meet people at events surrounding your shared interests, and be open to finding friends first. Also, don't forget your witchcraft. We witches have been given this wonderful and glorious Art to improve our lives and the lives of others. Why not use it to help yourself out of this painful situation?

"Instinct," "need," "urge," "craving,"—this is the level of devotion to an intention that is required of the witch who seeks magical success. Nothing else will do. This level of intensity can only be achieved through Desire. The horny lust that most men mistake for Desire is really just Passion turbo-charged by what the modern metaphysical community might call a "lack mentality."

The danger here is that this state of lack mimics Desire so closely that most people will simply confuse them and stop at Passion. Our modern Gay slang for horny people reveals this truth. Someone who wants sex too intensely is called "thirsty" or "hungry"—conditions associated with Desire earlier on in this chapter. In mimicking the signs of Desire, this Passion fools you into thinking that you have achieved something primal or necessary when you have barely scratched the surface.

Should you be able to identify true Desire from Passion and should you wish to apply it to a specific intention, you will need to understand one more thing to achieve success in casting a spell for love: How magic actually works.

8 HOW MAGIC WORKS: INTENTION & BELIEF

We talked about "wanting it bad enough" in the last chapter, but what does that mean? How does one know if he wants something "bad enough" to succeed at manifesting it into reality?

Let's start with a simple axiom that very few witches would debate: "Energy follows thought."

Even scientists are beginning to acknowledge this ancient wisdom about the power of thought. As we saw in the last chapter, however, regarding the faculty of Feeling, these mental states are not simple, easily defined things.

It is true that energy follows thought, but how exactly? Which part of thought? Which expression of the Thinking power is doing the actual work of directing the energy we raise through the Feeling faculty? Is it enough to merely "hope and pray" or must there be some level of concentration? If concentration is essential, why doesn't the magic work every time we concentrate on a specific goal?

In Feeling, we have the entirety of Emotion, and under Emotion's umbrella exists Affection, Passion, Desire, and countless other states of being. Presumably the same must be true for the faculties of Thinking and Willing as well. Which one of those aspects of thought are we talking about here and how does it interact with the Will?

Within the scope of Thinking, we have faculties like Reason, Imagination, Contemplation, Memory, Perception—and the list goes on. None of these qualities alone have the ability to direct the energy raised for magic.

While reason certainly has its benefits and rules over mundane life, it is actually more of a hindrance to magical success than a benefit. In fact, one of the biggest obstacles to a new witch's success in the Art Magical is his inability to shift away from the rational thought process into an ecstatic mindset.

Imagination is great, but it needs assistance to "make the magic go." Imagination certainly helps us to visualize a desired (or feared) outcome, which is necessary in a magical act, but without the element of Concentration, it's little more than a waste of time. Mental images disappear back into the ether as quickly as they emerged. How many disillusioned "dreamers" do we all know who never amount to anything? Conversely, concentrating on nothing may be great for meditation, but without a clearly defined idea of what you want to achieve, nothing happens. It's a bit like putting a car in neutral on a flat surface. So, as we explore these concepts in a very cursory way, it becomes apparent that neither Imagination nor Concentration alone is doing the heavy lifting to make the magic happen.

Memory is equally deficient in this regard. Sure, it pulls images and experiences from the past back into the present, which is extremely valuable, especially if you are trying to take stock of past successes or failures to either replicate the result or avoid a similar outcome. However, it often brings the energy to a screeching halt. How many people are so caught up in the past that they can't overcome their current struggles? Magic requires being in the present moment. Necessarily, Memory takes one out of the present moment and places him in another time entirely.

As for Perception, it is the source of a wealth of information for us, both mundane and magical. It is connected to both our physical and astral senses. However, its powers are mostly passive. Though it is highly involved in the passive powers of the witch (what have been identified as "psychic ability", namely, clairvoyance, clairaudience, and clairsentience), it does little to actually propel the active aspects of our Art, like casting spells.

The truth is that Thought alone does nothing to make the magic happen—neither do Feeling or Will alone. The mind must be fully exercised for the spark of magic to ignite, and this is the real power of Intention. It unifies the mind!

Intention alone engages the full scope of the mind, and it is the key to successfully "wanting something bad enough." The value of Intention to us, as witches, resides in the fact that it includes the full scope of the mind's powers: Belief, Desire, and a drive to achieve a contingent goal. A belief is merely a thought, which the thinker holds to be true. We have already gone into great detail on the nature of Desire in relation to the Feeling faculty, and that a drive to succeed is an aspect of Will requires no convincing for most people.

When witches talk about wanting something "bad enough," we mean to say that you must align and order your mental sphere in such a way that the chosen outcome is assured. That process begins with a staunch and firm knowing that your Truth has already become reality. Your Belief in this Truth needs to have the same force of conviction as your adherence to the Law of Gravity or any other natural law that you accept without question. During the period of time that you are casting the spell, you must buck all doubt and progress as if proof of your Truth was not only inevitable but had already come to light.

As Atkinson said, Desire is the highest crest of the wave of Feeling and Emotion, which is different than passion. It is not merely enough to lust for, want, or wish for something. You have to NEED that thing and be willing to bet everything on its attainment, like the man dying of thirst would risk his very life to quench that thirst. If your Desire doesn't reach the peak of life or death, if it doesn't touch something primal and essential on that level, you have not created the necessary battery to power the Intention.

This is one of the reasons that witches in the know talk about the importance of the sex drive to magical success. It has very little to do with the physical act of sex itself as we understand it today, which is to say that it has nothing to do with sex as recreation. Rather, it has everything to do with the sheer power of the innate and instinctual urge that all living things have to reproduce their genes. This power is so vast that it holds back the forces of Death and continues to populate the Earth in the face of decomposition and decay, which is why witches tap into it for our spells.

It is actually easier to achieve this level of Desire than you might think. Harnessing Desire for magical success starts with self-analysis. Notice how we are once again combining various mental elements to achieve our goal? In this case we're combining the power of Thinking through introspection and the power of Feeling through the specific desire in question.

Prioritizing Desires

1. Make a list of all your desires around love.

2. Once the list is complete, strike off the weakest of those desires. Anything that is merely temporary or passing should be removed now. Anything that will fail to bring you permanent and lasting satisfaction should fall into this list. For example, you don't want to give up saving for a house for a wild night out on the town. A home will serve you for years to come and provide long-term comfort and stability, while the night on the town will fly by with nothing to show for it but a lighter wallet.
3. Rank the remaining desires in order of importance to you, with no more than 3-5 strong and insistent desires remaining on the list.

At this point, you will become aware of a simple fact. As your list has grown smaller, your desires on that list have grown stronger in intensity. You are working with primal issues here: the love of mates. Because people are social animals and because companionship is essential to our species, this general realm of questioning naturally passes the Primal Test of the starving man seeking food or the man dying of thirst craving water. (If you should repeat this process for another set of desires, just make sure to pass that test before beginning the process of constructing your list.)

Take a break from your list. Turn your mind to other topics. Give it a chance to "percolate" through your subconscious for a week or so, then revisit the list.

When you come back to it, check your priorities again. Do you still order your desires in the same way? Has something changed? Did something else come up that needs to be added? Does it compete with or negate an item already on there? If so, decide between the two desires and prioritize the stronger one, eliminate the weaker.

Now make sure that the remaining desires are not contradictory or opposed to each other in some way. If any of them compete with another, remove the weaker one from your short list.

Once you have determined that the items on your list will

augment each other in the overarching theme of your grand design, it is time to begin working your magics on them.

Now that you have your short list of your strongest desires sorted out, it is time to begin ordering your life accordingly. This is where the Will power comes into play. The very first step in acquiring magical power is to take control of your mind. You must learn how to control your thoughts and command your moods.

9 MIRROR, MIRROR

Earlier, I quoted Plato referencing Diotima's wisdom about legacy and the desire for sex. To recapitulate, she said that our desire for sex stems from our fear of death, a desire to achieve immortality. No place is this fear of death more potent for Gay men than around the issues of aging. I address this concern here because it is one of the major impediments to manifesting a lasting, loving union for yourself.

Before I dive into this chapter, I want to be upfront. This is going to be brutal and raw. Some of the things I say may really upset you at first. It may sound like I am perpetuating unfortunate and even hateful opinions about older Gay men. If you are currently struggling with issues around growing older, you may be tempted to hear that I am saying you are obsolete, that you must resign yourself to being unattractive, that you are undeserving of love, or any of the countless other hateful things that are typically heard from some prominent segments of our community. I am not saying any of these things.

What I am doing, however, is pointing out in my own dramatic way (in order to draw attention to the issue) that many in the Gay Community hold these beliefs very sincerely. I'm highlighting that typical Gay Culture perpetuates these horrific standards and ideals and that it is very hard not to buy into them if your primary social network is made up of other Gay men within a stereotypical Gay environment.

Bear with me through the parts that make you angry. Reserve judging any one part of this chapter until you have read it in its entirety. I do have a theory that may present Gay men (at least Gay male witches) with a viable solution to get us out of this unfortunate predicament.

That said, how many Gay men believe that they are only lovable as long as they are pretty or young? If you're someone who holds that belief about yourself or about other Gay men, it is essential that you eliminate it from your mind as quickly as possible before attempting to draw a new partner into your life. It will only hamper your success and lead to heartache.

In the most mainstream segments of the Gay Community, youth is prized more highly than gold or silver. In fact, some Gay men genuinely believe that once they are no longer young enough or hot enough to make it in the Gay bars that their social lives are over. (In the era of the hookup app, this unfortunate misconception has been extended to all realms of Gay sex, not just the Gay bar.) Our ridiculous concept of "Gay death" at 30 is a prime example of this.

According to the Urban Dictionary, "When a Gay man turns 30, it's known as Gay Death." The implication is that the Gay man has aged out of his community. It also implies he is no longer hot enough for other Gay men to want to have sex with him, and, therefore, he should graciously walk off the dance floor and slink back into the shadows of oblivion, like Gerald Gardner expected Doreen Valiente to do when he wanted a younger High Priestess.

When I approached my own Gay death, I was downright suicidal. That is not hyperbole. I really did think about killing myself. I couldn't imagine turning 30 and not being married. I bought into Gay bar culture and even the hookup apps so much that I was totally convinced my dating life was over.

My poor coven and my family of origin had to suffer right along with me. For some of my friends, my experience turning 30 was the first time that they encountered something like this. My family had a similar example in the past, though it took them a while to connect the dots. Nearly all of my support network thought that it was the stupidest thing they had ever heard. Nobody could believe that I felt old at 30. Some of them even thought I was just being overly dramatic.

It didn't help that I wasn't shy about my angst or that I made no attempts to lessen anyone else's pain or frustration as they watched me suffer through it. How could I? I could barely get out of bed some days. I did hire a therapist, though, and I even went on anti-depressants for a little while. I actually preferred being dead to being single and 30.

During that period of my life, I thought a lot about my Aunt Jacki and the struggles she went through when she was unmarried and about to turn 30. She had died several years before this point in my life, so I couldn't get wisdom about my struggle from her directly. (At least I couldn't talk to her in any mundane, normally accepted way, and, truth be told, the idea of mediumship at that point was the furthest thing from my mind.) All I had was my memory of what she went through and how similar it seemed to what I was going through at the time.

Back when she was turning 30, she told the man that she was dating (the man who is now my uncle) that he had better marry her before she turned 30. There was no way she was going to become "an old maid." It sounds funny now, but she wasn't kidding at the time. She actually threatened to dump him and find another man who would make the commitment. The parallel between women and Gay men on this issue wasn't lost on me, but it was a few years before I would investigate the cause of this insecurity further.[66]

It wasn't long after I turned 30 that I realized how truly stupid the whole thing was. My 31st birthday was the best birthday of my entire life so far. Not only was I no longer 30, but I was in the best shape of my life. I was still hit on by men of all ages. 30 did nothing to ruin my sex life. Even the guys who said, "No one over 30" so clearly on their profiles, hit me up. When I not so politely pointed out that I didn't meet their age requirement, they responded back with something like "That doesn't apply to you. You're hot!"

Several Gay men have balked at my pointing out the existence of the concept of Gay Death. Guys over 30 have staunchly professed that they never experienced it and that the best years of their lives were after they turned 30. When I have brought this issue up in a crowd of older Gay men, some even try to "one up" the others by declaring that 40 or 50 or whatever "big" number year they can think of was better than even turning 30. In those situations, I politely refuse to point out the wisdom about professing too much. Gay men currently younger than 30 have also insisted that they have no issue with the big 3-0. I'm not saying that anyone I have personally talked to about this is lying. What I am saying, however, is that it is a widespread enough phenomenon to have made its way into the Urban Dictionary.

---

[66] Personally, I believe it has something to do with the Saturn Return, but that's a topic for another book.

Maybe some of the older Gay men did not have a problem turning any particular age. If so, I am genuinely overjoyed. As for Gay men under the age of 30, they haven't hit it yet, so only time will actually tell for them. What I do know is that I am not alone in having experienced this trial, and, whether or not anyone else wants to admit to it, it needs to be addressed here and now if only so that it can be wiped from existence once and for all.

The truth is that youth is prized very highly in the Gay Community, but it takes a back seat to beauty, especially if that beautiful older Gay man has maintained a certain level of strength and vitality. The phobia around aging that Gay men suffer has less to do with growing old than it does with the perceived loss of our seductive powers.

To see that this is true, simply look at the fictional witches who hold sway over the collective Gay male imagination. In the television adaptation of George R. R. Martin's *Game of Thrones*, Melisandre, the Red Priestess, who is older than dirt but manages to maintain her beauty through a glamoured necklace, has as many Gay male fans as the young, sexy Daenerys Targaryen. Michelle Pfeiffer steals the show as the ancient witch Lamia in the movie version of Neil Gaiman's book *Stardust*. When she eats the heart of a previously fallen star and regains "the glory of her youth," she becomes iconic. Who can forget that seductive look over her shoulder as she ogles herself in the mirror? Lucy Lawless, who played Countess Palatine, Ingrid von Marburg on WGN America's television show *Salem*, received rave reviews from critics and fans alike for her portrayal of this ancient and powerful witch. The Countess was described as "a beautiful woman who appears to be in her late 40s" on The Salem Wiki page.[67] Not merely a supporting character to the younger Mary Sibley played by Janet Montgomery, the Countess retains her beauty and grace even when placed side-by-side with the lead starlet. In American Horror Story Coven, Marie Laveau had Gay men on the edge of their seats rooting for her throughout the entire season. Though she is immortal, she did not stop the aging process in her youth, nor did she revert back to a more youthful time in her life. In fact,

---

[67] https://salem.fandom.com/wiki/Countess_Von_Marburg

like Lamia and the Countess, she appears to be a beautiful woman over the age of 40, but her seductive allure eclipsed the younger female witches on the show. The list could go on for pages, but you get the idea.

The bottom line here is that Gay men are offended by "old," "decrepit," and "decaying" flesh, but there is something magical about being ancient as the hills. In truth, ancient beauty is even more captivating to us than youthful beauty as we saw with the witches from pop culture just mentioned. There is just something about being "ageless" that truly fascinates us, and is the key to overcoming the Peter Pan complex that currently haunts our community.

Unfortunately, all examples of these "ancient beauties" belong exclusively to women. Conversely, the traditional imagery of aging men always seems to depict someone knowledgeable, understanding, maybe even enlightened, who possesses a philosophical or rational wisdom. He is often portrayed as pretentious and even a bit comical. He is the counselor, the scholar, the wise fool, the Sage—a de-sexualized supporting character who aids younger men in their quests to achieve glory and honor. Merlin, Gandalf, Dumbledore—none of these old men are ever viewed to be sexually viable, like their Crone counterparts. The outcry over J. K. Rowling's revelation that Dumbledore was actually Gay is a prime example of this phenomenon. Merlin is sometimes paid lip service in modern adaptations, but when that happens, he is invariably depicted as "young Merlin" and is made into the main character of the story. He no longer fulfills the Sage role in these depictions. Rather, he is working on developing the wisdom and experience he demonstrates later on when he actually becomes the Sage we all know so well. That's really not the same thing.

As for the de-sexualized aspect of the Sage,[68] one might be tempted to argue that it is common knowledge that women just grow old, but men grow "distinguished." This is nothing more than hype, spin, and delusion. If you doubt this, take any man who looks like Sean Connery (the archetypal image used most often to validate this "distinguished" nonsense) and compare him to someone like Jane Fonda. The two actors are roughly the same age, both in their 80s. If you still want to stand your ground on the "distinguished" argument, imagine taking both of them to any Gay bar in America. Jane Fonda would be adored, worshipped, and guys would crowd around her in awe of her glamour and beauty. Sean Connery, if he weren't rich and famous, would be laughed at or, more likely, simply ignored.

The truth is that the Sage, as an archetype of masculinity, really doesn't belong to Gay men. Outside of the desexualization argument about the Sage, when a Gay man attempts to assume the Sage's mantle, it is always seen as a perversion of the role. Consider characters like Jafar in *Aladdin*, who, for the record, is desexualized in the story. Fan fiction talks about Jafar being Gay, and Disney certainly played up his "Gay mannerisms," but that was a demonized and laughable version of Gay, not a sexualized one. It actually serves more to harm our public image than help it. While Gay Sage-like characters may be viewed to be powerful (even magical), they are not viewed to be wise. Instead, their claim to Sage status, if there is one at all, resides in their cunning, which aside from being more Feminine in quality also has negative connotations outside of Craft circles. For the record, the reason that *Cunning* has negative associations outside of our Craft circles and is revered within them is precisely because it is a Feminine mental quality, which belongs to the Crone. Any way you slice it,

---

[68] I am not alone in pointing out how the Sage is desexualized. Some scholars, like some of the sources quoted in Joanne Sienko Ott's thesis, have even argued that the definition of Sage has no gender bias whatsoever, that it is a role that can apply as equally to woman as to men. While in Wicca we do tend to think of the Sage as the final stage of manhood, there are certainly examples of other esoteric traditions that back up this theory. The most readily accessible examples that spring to the forefront of the Western mind, are Taoist, Yogic, and Tantric sages. While certainly less numerous than their male counterparts, there are more than ample numbers of women who qualify for this role.

whenever a Gay (or presumably Gay) male attempts to fill the Sage's shoes, it is always a bastardization of the older Straight man's respected role.

Which brings us to the next point. Part of the Sage's role is that he serve as a respected counselor to the hero. In order to claim his counselor role, he must first have been respected for his own accomplishments in the past. The most important role within this stage of life, the place where the Sage's advice is most crucial is in counseling younger men on issues of navigating manhood with wisdom. As a counselor, he must be willing to step off the main stage of his own story and be relegated to a supporting role in someone else's story. In myth, he must be willing to help a younger man achieve glory and prestige. In real life, he must offer insight into the Male condition from the benefit of his knowledge and experience. If he refuses to be minimized or can't contribute in this way (either because he lacks the wisdom or the younger men don't recognize it in him), there is no hope for him. He will simply be overlooked and forgotten, and life will move on without him.

In order to step off the main stage, though, the Sage must have first occupied space in that spotlight. He must have been viewed to have been a major player on the stage of life. For Jafar to have really qualified for the Sage title, he would first had to have worn Aladdin's shoes, i.e. been the hero of the tale. He must have been seen as a "real man." The sad truth is that, outside of fringe movies or cult classics reserved exclusively for Gay male audiences, Gay men are never the main players or the heroes of the story. In this case, art really does mirror life.

As the song says, *It's A Man's World*, and it is: a Straight man's world. When the wisdom of the Sage can only be appreciated after the man has achieved success or built a legacy of his own, a necessary prerequisite of the role is that he have been in a position of power before achieving old age. No one claims the doddering, old codger is worth listening to. He is laughed off and ignored. However, the line between Sage and doddering, old codger is hair thin.

While the wisdom and eccentricity of the solitary, cranky, old wizard may seem appealing on the surface to some, this is not the essential part of the Sage Role. It is not the quintessential quality that makes him a Sage. I don't know many Gay men who would be content to ascribe the Sage's actual role to themselves as they age. In fact, regarding the desexualized component, the opposite seems to be more the case. Rather than becoming less sexual as we age, many Gay men seem to have an unrepressed sexual desire that reasserts itself well into their 50s, 60s, and beyond. The statistics on Cialis and Viagra sales within the Gay Community should be enough to prove that particular point. As for being accomplished men who were looked up to for their masculinity or other "manly" virtues, though we certainly have them, society is still a long way off from recognizing this fact on any real or meaningful level. Since we not only lack respect as men but are actually outright demonized, we also fail to accomplish the requirement of being able to give counsel around issues of navigating manhood with wisdom.

Truthfully, Gay men have much more in common with women then we do with Straight men, especially when it comes to issues of aging. The demonization aspect mentioned above is a prime example. If you doubt this, look at the names they use to ridicule us. Both Gay men and women are demonized by society at large. When a woman refused to be subservient or she was in some other way uncontrollable, they called her a "witch," and, if she was old or ugly, they called her "Crone" or "hag." Gay men are called "faggot" or "fairy"—two terms that are heavily tied to witchcraft. The faggot was a collection of sticks or a pyre. Witches were burned alive on such pyres. The connection between fairies and witches is self-explanatory and I need not go into further detail here. The demonization of Gay men is actually two-fold. We are not only emasculated, we are also feminized in the eyes of the typical Straight man and, because he reigns down over everyone else, we are also looked down upon by society at large. It is in this feminization where they demonize us, because, truth be told, the demonization of Gay men, is misogyny pure and simple.

Women are held to a higher standard of beauty than Straight men,[69] and so are Gay men. I would love to say that we are beyond having to hear the childhood wisdom of "don't judge a book by

---

[69] Dare I say IMPOSSIBLE standard?

its cover," but a large portion of the Gay Community (and Society in general) still needs to hear it. As sad as this is to say, no older, single Gay man could look like Sean Connery and still realistically expect to get laid from a purely sexual experience within the standard Gay Community without having to pay for it.[70] Gay men are required to maintain an unrealistic standard of beauty within the mainstream currents of our community, and just like women, we are shamed for it when we don't succeed at that impossible task. Straight men can "let themselves go" and still realistically expect to find a mate 20, 30, 40 years younger than themselves. This double standard is how the "distinguished" delusion came about in the first place. It happens all the time. There are privileges to being male that most Gay men simply don't get afforded within either the Gay Community or overarching society.

Aging Gay men and women also share more in common with each other than just demonization and unrealistic standards of beauty being enforced on us by the societies in which we live. While reviewing the literature on the Sage and Crone archetypes, Joanne Sienko Ott points out that the styles of wisdom associated with the Sage and Crone are fundamentally different. The Sage's way of knowing stems from reason and logic. The Crone's wisdom, however, is more intuitive and relational, based on insights, feelings, and creativity.[71]

The Crone's style of wisdom is more aligned with the stereotypical depictions of the way that Gay men think than the Sage's method. Traditional depictions of Gay men back this up. We are viewed to be creative, intuitive, and having emotional intelligence, which are all qualities listed in association with the

---

[70] Of course, there are subsets of the community that aren't this shallow. (That's true of every group.) Gay male witches, for example, tend to be a little less dismissive around old age than the traditional Gay Community. There are even some individual Gay men who do not suffer from this prejudice scattered across various sectors of our Gayborhood. However, because this book is written to heal the entire Gay Community, it is necessary to admit that the bulk of Gay men (even older Gay men) fall into this ageist category.

[71] Ott, Joanne Sienko. *The Crone Archetype: Women Reclaim Their Authentic Self By Resonating with Crone Imagery.* MA Thesis. SOPHIA, 2011. https://sophia.stkate.edu/ma_hhs/17/, p. 14.

Crone, not the Sage.

The big difference between women and Gay men in the issue of aging is that women's menstrual blood dries up, whereas Gay men don't have a specific point in their stage of life where they lose the ability to ejaculate. Some men suffer ED in later life or lose the ability to have sex for health reasons, but that is by no means an inevitable bridge that all gay men must cross. Some men maintain their sexual vitality until the day they die. Menstrual blood and semen bear similar weights in terms of sexual potency and metaphysical power.

Joanne Sienko Ott, quoting Barbara Walker in her thesis, says, "In ancient times the Mensa symbolized the lunar 'wise blood' and it was believed that women entering the third stage of life (postmenopausal) kept their wisdom within."[72] The internalizing of these potent life-giving energies empower the Crone and grant her the ability to throw off all the shackles that have held her back up to that point in her life, should she choose. I also believe that, in addition to redirecting women's sexual energies away from birthing the next generation, Dame Nature was wise to conserve what remained of the Crone's life force within the body. I have a theory that it is this act of conservation combined with the Crone's brand of wisdom, which makes the big difference in the way that women age compared to the way that most men age.

Though the Crone archetype also fails to fit Gay men exactly, it is closer to the truth than the Sage for those of us who wish to remain sexually viable and appealing to other partners well into our later lives. If the Gay man in question is content to be approached as a non-sexual, wise, old counselor, the mantle of the Sage role will fit just fine. However, in my own personal experience dealing with Gay men, I know very few single Gay men who would willingly embrace that fate without turning bitter, jaded, or vengeful in the process.

The truth is that, like countless tribal cultures have proven throughout history, Gay men are on a path all our own—neither completely aligned with the male nor female paths but running

---

[72] Ott, Joanne Sienko. *The Crone Archetype: Women Reclaim Their Authentic Self By Resonating with Crone Imagery.* MA Thesis. SOPHIA, 2011. https://sophia.stkate.edu/ma_hhs/17/, p. 14-15.

parallel to them both at different times. In my opinion, we need a better title for this stage of a Gay man's life than Sage. We need an archetype that gives a sense of dignity through the aging process without castrating us during it, so that older Gay men can have hope and stop living in fear that aging is synonymous with "decaying."

Should Gay men wish to replicate a process similar to what women experience as they age and become more like Jane Fonda than Sean Connery, we are in a good position to do so.[73] First, we already have a link to the Crone archetype in the way that we think and the style of our wisdom. Second, as I said in *Garbed In Green*, we have access to a vast amount of power potential within our bodies that remains largely untapped by the bulk of Gay men. We have but to access it and direct our thoughts according to this purpose. Finally, we also have the ability to conserve our own life forces within ourselves to a greater or lesser extent in accordance with our desire for longevity. This is what the next chapter is all about.

---

[73] Let's acknowledge the plastic surgery argument here. Undoubtedly it has a part to play. However, Sean Connery and Jane Fonda have both had plastic surgery. Writing this theory off because of medical intervention is disingenuous. The truth is that if there weren't something else going on energetically in addition to the surgeries, the difference between the two would not be so glaring.

10 SEX & REGENERATIVE POWER

As I discussed in the previous chapter, the average Gay man prizes youth and struggles with aging. I'd like to point out the wisdom of applying Sybil Leek's Tenet of Humility here. It is always wise to accept Nature's course and our place within it. The truth is that the material plane is constantly cycling through periods of growth and decay. The seasons are a wonderful and non-threatening example of this recurring theme. We, as organic beings, are not immune to these cycles, and eventually everyone must face the ravages of time. However, that doesn't do any good in helping living, breathing Gay men address their current fears around growing older and "aging out" of their communities.

The truth is that we can't stop Time from marching onward. We are all going to leave youth behind us and mature, but that does not mean that we must become decrepit in the wake of Time's procession. With some knowledge, forethought, and diligence, we can stop Time from trampling all over our faces and ravaging our bodies. This chapter is an introduction on how to begin doing just that.

After all, one of the undisputed powers of the witch is to make the ugly beautiful. As witches, we know that energy follows thought. We saw exactly how thought, specifically belief, influences energy and magic in an earlier chapter of this book. As people living in the modern era, we also have the benefit of scientific advancement to augment our occult knowledge. We now know that matter is really nothing more than energy arranged in a certain way. Therefore, it stands to reason that our thoughts can impact our bodies just the same as they can impact the rest of our realities. We only need to believe that they can.

Atkinson discusses this very topic in his book *Regenerative Power or Vital Rejuvenation*. Starting with an uncontroversial version of this theory, he says, "It is a matter of common knowledge that the secretion of the gastric and intestinal juices is largely augmented by the sight or even the thought and imaginative images of appetizing food."[74] Basically, the sight, even the thought of food can start the digestive processes. "Moreover," he says, "it is a matter of common experience among human beings that suggestions concerning delicious foods 'make the mouth water,' and cause the appetite to manifest itself."[75]

Atkinson references another unarguable fact by pointing out that the very presence of an infant, especially a baby's cries, can cause a nursing mother to lactate instantaneously. He also makes note that "Certain strong emotions, particularly those of fright, will cause the secretion of chemical substances which will produce an evacuation of the bowels—an artificially induced diarrhea."[76] There is no end to the examples of these phenomena, which science has catalogued over the centuries.

Remember, simply shutting your eyes tight, crossing your fingers, and wishing something to be true isn't real belief. It certainly isn't the type of belief that we are talking about when witches discuss magical success. Charles Sanders Pierce probably said it best when he said, "The essence of belief is the establishment of a habit; and different beliefs are distinguished by the different modes of action to which they give rise." Real belief requires action, the application of principles in a habitual way that produce long-lasting effects. Nowhere is this truer than in the witch's anti-aging powers.

Atkinson points out that it "has been proved that fear, anger, and especially jealousy, produce secretions which tend to poison the system; while cheerfulness, hopeful and inspiring mental states are seen to induce secretions which act as a physical tonic.

"It is a matter of common experience, and of scientific record," he continues, "that sad and depressing emotional states, long

---

[74] Atkinson, W. W. and Edward E. Beals. *Regenerative Power or Vital Rejuvenation.* Robert Collier Book Corp, 1975, 133.

[75] Atkinson, W. W. and Edward E. Beals. *Regenerative Power or Vital Rejuvenation.* Robert Collier Book Corp, 1975, 133.

[76] Atkinson, W. W. and Edward E. Beals. *Regenerative Power or Vital Rejuvenation.* Robert Collier Book Corp, 1975, 134.

continued, tend to bring about a state of ill-health, lessened vitality, and even ultimate death; these physiological processes now being known to result directly from the presence and action of toxic secretions in the blood. On the other hand, it is as well known that the emotional states of successful love, certainty or strong hope of success in business or social undertakings, etc., will produce a marked improvement in the general health of the individual, in some cases almost 'working a miracle' in his physical condition."[77]

It is important to note some key elements of this quote. Certain "long continued" emotional states, whether positive or negative, can have drastic effects on our physical bodies. No one emotion in any one moment is going to wreak havoc on your health (or heal you of disease either). However, over time, consistent application of a positive or negative state of mind will produce drastic results for good or ill. This is one of the reasons that so many elders within the Craft talk about witches growing more beautiful as they age or growing haggard before their time, depending on how they "use their powers."

In order to apply this witch's power for rejuvenation, you must start with your own mental state and make it a habit to have a "positive attitude" toward life as often as possible. Again, meditation will help tremendously here, but that is not enough. You must extend your habits of belief into your mundane world as well.

That is actually where the best magics start: with the mundane tasks, which surround your goal. If you want a better job, put together your resume and set up some interviews before you cast your spells. If you want to buy a house, spend some time strengthening your credit score or, better yet, save up the actual cash to buy the house outright.

If you want to maintain a youthful, strong, and vital appearance that makes you look ageless despite how many rotations of the sun you've actually seen, then eat right, take care of your skin, and workout. Do yoga. Lift weights. Take up running. Exercise! Get

---

[77] Atkinson, W. W. and Edward E. Beals. *Regenerative Power or Vital Rejuvenation*. Robert Collier Book Corp, 1975, 134-135.

your body moving and keep it moving.

Remember Newton's First Law of Motion: "A body at rest will remain at rest, and a body in motion will remain in motion unless it is acted upon by an external force." When bodies stop moving, they decay and, eventually, die. To see that this is true, simply look at someone who retires, sells the family home, and moves into a rancher. The simple acts of giving up climbing the stairs to the bedroom and spending most of the day on the couch watching TV instead of being active produces rapid aging results. A previously vital 64-year old is now decrepit and has one foot in the grave only a few years after retirement. As a witch, if I wanted to reinvigorate that person, I might do nothing else but convince him to sell his rancher and buy a townhouse where his bedroom was on the second floor. That one simple act alone would produce remarkable results in a very short time.

After the mundane tasks of taking care of the physical health of our bodies have been tended to, some attention must be given to the way in which we engage sexually with ourselves and other people. Sex is a source of immense power. As witches, we revel in this fact. Many of our rites, like Beltane, are built off it.

Atkinson quotes an anonymous writer as saying, "The ancient occultists recognized the wonderful power stored in the reproductive organism, which is given out not only in the act of actual reproduction and procreation, but which may also be dissipated in the unnatural excesses and practices to which the race is addicted."[78] They soon discovered that this wonderful concentrated power could be used not only for the purposes of generation, but also for the purpose of re-generation of the life activities within one's own body, the exhaustion of which occurs if the vital forces be given out in procreation or waste."[79] Basically, if we conserve our sexual energies, we can use them to heal ourselves and preserve our own vitality while increasing

---

[78] He's basically saying that people are horny little devils.

[79] Atkinson, W. W. and Edward E. Beals. *Regenerative Power or Vital Rejuvenation.* Robert Collier Book Corp, 1975, 75-76.

longevity.[80]

In its most extreme form, this advice can be taken as advocating celibacy, but there are certainly less ascetic paths, which will still yield near "miraculous" results for the witch who wishes to preserve "the dewiness of his youth." Atkinson goes on to say, "If men were to think and speak of Sex just as of any other natural function, then all the mystery would fall from it, and also all the exaggerated worship of it on the one hand and the exaggerated fear and dread of it on the other hand."[81] You do not have to give up sex to enjoy the benefits talked about by these ancient occultists.

I know many of you may be struggling with this concept. A dear friend of mine certainly did when I mentioned it to him. In fact, he fought me tooth and nail, and pitched the worst fit you can possibly imagine, but, then, fate intervened.

While vacationing in Vancouver, he injured his lower back and was bedridden for the better part of a week, suffering from terrible spasms. His pain was so severe that he couldn't even stand or sit in a chair.

One night, his partner was in need of sexual relief, and my friend was craving the intimacy of that moment even though he could not get release of his own. So, he begrudgingly made use of the River of Rejuvenation exercise shown below. Imagine his surprise and chagrin, when he had to call me the next day and admit that it worked. Not only did it calm his sexual desires, but, over the next few days, he began to see significant and measurable improvements in the health of his back. Medical professionals had informed him that the condition would take five to six weeks to heal, but using the River of Rejuvenation exercise for just one week, he decreased the healing time by a month.

Should you wish to maintain your own vitality, you do have to approach sex in a healthier way than the average Gay man might be accustomed to doing. As witches, we know that other people

---

[80] *Longevity* is often a euphemism for retaining attributes of youthfulness well into old age in a great many of the occult texts on this subject.

[81] Atkinson, W. W. and Edward E. Beals. *Regenerative Power or Vital Rejuvenation*. Robert Collier Book Corp, 1975, 148.

can sap our energies in many ways. It's a common complaint from empathetic people that they often feel emotionally drained at the end of the day or after they've been in a crowded space. Everyone knows at least one person who likes to pick a fight just so he can get attention. Unfortunately, most people don't make the connection between these common, everyday occurrences and the fact that sex does exactly the same thing.

Sex is an energetic exchange, just like all other forms of human interaction. Certain subsets of the Gay Community frequently discuss this phenomenon. Most notably, the Gay BDSM Culture of the '80s and '90s talked about this. However, few people today make the leap of logic that comes next.

If sex is an energetic exchange, then, as witches who wish to preserve our own vitality, we ought to vet our sexual partners more carefully. If someone is depressed and I have sex with him, not only will he drain me of my own vigor, but he will also pass some measure of his negative emotional state onto me. Remember two things. First, Nature abhors a vacuum. Second, Emotions are Feelings, and Feelings are the "agreeable or disagreeable phase of a mental state." As we saw in Chapter 4 while talking about Thoughtform Elementals, Thoughts can be infectious if they are powerful enough. The same is true of people who abuse drugs or alcohol. People who find their refuge from the world in drugs or by abusing alcohol have reached such a deep state of despair that they are actually the spiritual and energetic equivalent of being syphilitic. Engage with them sexually, and you risk infection.

Despite the average Gay man's insistence to the contrary, sex is not a handshake. To be fair, a handshake is also an energetic exchange, but the difference between sex and a handshake is an order of magnitude. From a handshake, you might get a little of someone else's "ick" on you, but it is bound to be minor enough to deal with easily and effortlessly most of the time. Sex, on the other hand, is so much more intimate. The energies that are exchanged are not only personal, but they are also mingled thoroughly between the different partners involved. Sexual energies are one of the most powerful that Dame Nature could create. They have to fight off the unassailable forces of decay and Death while continuing to populate the material plane. Add to that already immense power battery a negative mental state, like the despair of someone who is hiding from life by abusing drugs or alcohol, and you can create a real living nightmare for yourself. I believe this is one of the reasons that the standard Gay Hookup Culture is the way it is.

None of this information is intended to shame the person who struggles with a drug or alcohol addiction. Nor is this about compounding the problem that someone who suffers from clinical depression goes through. These are very real conditions, and the people who grapple with them deserve compassion and respect. However, respecting the individual and treating him compassionately does not amount to the same thing as "getting down in the trenches with him" and sacrificing yourself before the onslaught of his untreated condition.

More than just being an energetic exchange though, the sex force within the human body can and does do so many remarkable things. It is one of the great sins of the "Moral Majority" and the Christian accession in general that we have hidden this fact from the general public. Children are barely even taught about the procreative powers of sex. Instead, they are led to dismiss these things as "sinful," and, if they are not outright terrified by their first explorations of their own sexuality, they are shamed when they inevitably give into those "temptations." Even in the most liberal schools, teachers are afraid to talk openly about sex with children for fear of "corrupting" them in some way or being seen as somehow abusing these children or "robbing them of their innocence."

Even adults who are otherwise well-educated often find their knowledge around sex deficient. I remember one night back in college when some friends and I were hanging out drinking and playing one of those card games that "get the conversation going." Invariably the topic of sex came up, and, though I'm not sure how we wound up talking about "women peeing," I'll never forget all the fantastical misconceptions some of the Gay men at the party had about women's bodies.

Several of the women pressed these guys on the issue. They genuinely couldn't believe that grown adults lacked this basic information about human anatomy. In response, one Gay guy said, very matter-of-factly, "I'm gold star, bitch." Then, one-by-one, all the other guys who were beginning to recognize the deficiency in their own understanding of the female body began flashing their credentials, trying to one-up each other.

"I'm not just gold star. I'm platinum!"

One guy took it up a notch and said, "I hate vagina's so much, I was born cesarean." Then there was some hysterical pantomiming about bracing oneself in a X position, trying to fight gravity and refusing to budge until the doctors cut him out.

Finally, after watching all this nonsense, one woman just got frustrated enough that she took one of the "gold star Gays" to the bathroom and taught him about the "birds and the bees." Needless-to-say, he came squealing out a few moments later, and we all sort of just laughed it off.

When the basics of human sexuality are denied to entire generations of people, is it any wonder that the more complex applications of the sex force are also concealed? Most people don't know that if the vital energies of sex are retained within the body, even for a brief period, that the brain becomes more efficient, the nerves steady themselves, even the muscles benefit from the accumulation of this potent force. Doubt that this is true? Consider the habit of athletes who abstain from sex before a big game. This occult wisdom is the source of that commonly held practice.

Science backs up the athlete's superstition, by the way. Atkinson says, "It [Science] holds that the sex-glands of the male and female secrete certain elements which make for the invigoration of the mental and physical nature of the man or woman …".[82] Over the last 50 years or so, vast amounts of research have been conducted into physiology and the effects of these glands on the human body.

The ductless glands, in general, have been found to secrete substances that are of the highest value to the health of the body. The thyroid regulates the body's metabolic rate. The pituitary gland regulates growth, metabolism and body composition. The adrenal glands are vital to life. They help regulate the metabolism,

---

[82] Atkinson, W. W. and Edward E. Beals. *Regenerative Power or Vital Rejuvenation.* Robert Collier Book Corp, 1975, 64-65.

control blood pressure, and aid the body in responding to stress.

The genital glands, in particular, can benefit the overall health of the body. Atkinson says, "Advanced modern physiology has at least tentatively advanced the theory that the Genital Glands, particularly the Testes and the Ovaries, not only produce the primary reproductive cells, but that they also secrete other substances of a high potency which are believed to exert a strong influence not only upon the growth and development of the embryo after the ovum has been fertilized by the sperm, but also upon the growth and development of the body of the individual in whose Genital Glands they have been secreted."[83] Speaking plainly, Atkinson is saying that the secretions of the genital glands can be used to augment the physical body of the individual, not just reproduce other bodies.

In addition to the sperm and seminal fluid, the genital glands also produce *internal secretions*. "Internal Secretions are substances elaborated in Ductless Glands and discharged directly into the blood; they are substances secreted by animal organs or tissues which preside over the development, growth, reproduction, and the chemical regulation of the body."[84] In the male, the most well-known of these internal secretions is testosterone.

The benefits of retaining these vital forces within oneself are not limited to efficiency and vibrant health. Beauty is another byproduct of the ancient practice of semen retention, which is really what Atkinson and other occultists like him are discussing. After a consistent practice of retaining one's sexual force, the eyes begin to brighten, and other individual features begin to take on a more pleasing appearance. Indeed, the entire face becomes more attractive for this effort. For the Gay male witch who wishes to thwart Time, he could do no better than to reduce the frequency with which he ejaculates.

I am not advocating that you give up sex. Nor am I advocating that you give up ejaculation entirely. The truth is that ejaculation

---

[83] Atkinson, W. W. and Edward E. Beals. *Regenerative Power or Vital Rejuvenation.* Robert Collier Book Corp, 1975, 97.

[84] Atkinson, W. W. and Edward E. Beals. *Regenerative Power or Vital Rejuvenation.* Robert Collier Book Corp, 1975, 98.

is a wonderful way to regulate the body's hormones. I am merely advocating that IF you want to practice the internal alchemy that will help you become ageless, you should learn to regulate your own internal chemistry in accordance with your desire.

Should you wish to practice this alchemical form of regeneration, you have merely to do three things. First, reduce the frequency with which you ejaculate. Atkinson refers to this, in his wonderfully Victorian way, as a "sane and rational temperance in the matter of expenditure of the sex energies."[85] It's worth noting here that each of us must determine for ourselves what an appropriate balance of these "expenditures" might look like. Second, direct your psychic powers towards enhancing the normal production of the internal secretions of the genital glands for the purposes of physical and mental reinvigoration, recuperation, and revitalization. Finally, employ your psychic abilities to distribute these sexual energies throughout the body.

The River of Rejuvenation

Before beginning this practice, abstain from sexual pleasure for at least 3 days and refrain from seeking release during the entirety of the time that you are engaged in this practice. This exercise can be used to calm the passions as well as reclaim the internal secretions of the genital glands. My advice is start small. Begin by only doing this meditation two days. Then resume your normal sexual activities for a week or so. After another 3-day break, try this meditation for no more than 4 days. Then resume sexual activity for another week or so. When you attempt the third round, try this exercise for no more than a week before resuming your normal sexual activity again. If you see benefit from this practice, you can always try it again later for another 7-day stint.

For the first couple months, do not try to extend your practice longer than one week at a time. Be gentle with yourself and see how your body reacts to the exercise. If you are able to consistently experience healthy, positive results from this practice, you may want to investigate a deeper study of internal alchemy

---

[85] Atkinson, W. W. and Edward E. Beals. *Regenerative Power or Vital Rejuvenation*. Robert Collier Book Corp, 1975, 142.

and find a teacher who can help you take this practice safely to the next level.

In this exercise, we are going to enhance these potent energies with a brief meditative practice by using the imagery of a mountain spring that feeds a mighty river. This imagery represents increasing the flow of these secretions and their absorption by the body. Calm your mind and set the intention to enhance your body's normal production of these internal genital secretions.

Take a few deep breaths and spend a moment or two clearing your mind. Focus on your root chakra and see the image of the mountain spring. Notice how this spring is connected to a river. Take note of its force and flow. As you breathe in and out, visualize the spring begin to gush. See the force and flow of the spring increase, and see the river begin to swell. Watch as it overflows its banks and spills out onto the land around it. As you inhale, see the land begin to absorb the overflow until the water has seeped into the ground. Then see the fields become fertile. See a veritable harvest of plenty appear in the field. Affirm for yourself that the bounty of the land is directly proportionate to your success in this endeavor; and take comfort in the fact that you are harvesting the fruits of your labor even as you sit in quiet contemplation.

This exercise is useful for retaining the sexual force within the body. You can use it to calm the passions or accumulate sexual force for magical purposes through temporary sexual fasting.

Bottom line: Age is for wine and cheese.

11 IN PRAISE OF A HOOKUP

Terry Pratchett said it best, "When you break rules, break 'em good and hard."

Up until this point in my books, I have been rather down on the concept of hookups and careless sex. In truth, there is nothing wrong with either a hookup or casual sex. Just because a Gay man is single, doesn't mean that he should have to endure unwanted celibacy if he can find a willing partner.

However, as I said in the Sex and Regenerative Power Chapter, indiscriminate casual sex can sap one's vitality. Rather than hemorrhaging this power all over the room, witches and occultists in the know encourage discrimination combined with wise, healthy choices around sex. Just because you are turned on by every Tom, Dick, and Harry does not mean that you must, or should, jump into bed with him.

The question to ask is this: Will this experience help replenish your storehouse of magnetism and vital energy or will the encounter deplete your reserves? Sometimes sex with a loving partner is exactly what's called for to do the trick. Alternatively, a fair exchange of energy between two strangers who are approaching the situation from an honest, straightforward, and understanding perspective is exactly what's called for.

My big problem with the way that Hookup Culture works in the bulk of the Gay Community is that it encourages us to be predatory and to drain each other of our vitality. The abuses of both parties are so numerous that I could write an entire book just on that subject. Rather than healing or uplifting each other with sex, which is certainly possible, the average Gay man caught up in hookup culture is desperately trying to fix something broken within himself.

That said, I cannot deny that one of the biggest elements of my own healing around issues of sexual and emotional abuse came from a hookup. As I was writing this book, I constantly experimented with myself. I tried out the things I recommended. I did my own rituals. I even explored theories that were opposite to my own in order to see if I was wrong or something else might work better than what I was proposing. As much as it pains me to give any credit or credence to any part of hookups, I must concede that not all hookups are bad.

I met Danny[86] four years ago, during my first time living in North Carolina. We both lived in Durham, and found each other on Grindr. I was just out of another relationship, and was struggling with my own guilt and shame at having failed yet again. In truth, I was throwing myself a pity party and being rather pathetic about it all. I should not have been on the apps seeking a sexual partner in the first place.

I say that because sex is an energy raising tool, and, as I said in the chapter, How Magic Works: Intention & Belief, energy follows thought. I was empowering my own "demons" of guilt and shame. It really would have been better for me to seek therapy and move on from the pain, but that is not what I did.

I got lucky when I encountered Danny. He was kind and patient with me. We didn't just fuck. We talked.

After the sex was over, he didn't just usher me out the door. We spent time having actual conversations. We told each other about our lives. Sometimes we just talked about our days. Though we never quite became friends, we were friendly with each other.

When I moved up to Pennsylvania, we kept in touch from time to time. I would get quick texts letting me know he was thinking about me or that he missed me, or I would write him just to say "hi." It was nothing serious or extremely deep, but it was nice nonetheless.

Since I was single when I left Pennsylvania, I made a point of reaching out to Danny before I made the move, and, not surprisingly, he was overjoyed. "Wow that's great news!" he said. "Did you just need a change?"

I explained that I had written a book and was moving back to North Carolina to be with some of the witches in my tradition. (As I said, we talked after sex. Since we talked about my spirituality, Danny already knew a great deal about some of this stuff.)

---

[86] Yes! I changed his name to protect his identity.

At the time, North Carolina had the highest number of initiated Gala witches in any one state. There were two covens that, combined, comprised nearly half the tradition, and no local Elders to support them.

The Pennsylvania coven where I was High Priest had two second degree initiates who were in a working pair relationship with each other (we call them *Anam Caras* in Gala), and they were ready to step up and run the group. Plus, they had two Elders within 20 miles of their covenstead. If they needed local support, they would always have it, and I was only ever a phone call away for them. There was very little left for me to do for Gala in Pennsylvania, but the North Carolina covens were at a crucial stage in their developments, and they needed support. So, I moved.

To my surprise, Danny not only knew about my book; he had bought a copy of it and actually read it! We talked about it for a while. Apparently, he liked it. He had some really interesting questions, and wanted to know more about my thoughts and experiences behind the book. All-in-all, this portion of our conversation took up two or three days of intermittent texting.

Danny is like that. He isn't only about the sex. For him, it's always been about the connection. Even when the sex is casual or may only happen the one time, he still wants it to be a good experience for both parties. Like I said, I was lucky to find him when I did, especially considering the bad head space I was in at the time.

Honestly, it took me a while to get used to that. The vast majority of my other hookups before him just wanted me to leave after they were done. When they got off, it was over. All the passion and intensity were shut off as quickly as one might turn out a light. Danny, on the other hand, actually pulled me into him and cuddled. He kissed my neck and pressed his torso against my back. It was intimate, tender, and sweet, like lovers basking in each other's presence even though we were very nearly strangers.

Our first real conversation after sex actually revolved around my discomfort with the intimacy he tried to show me. I explained how other guys had discarded me like yesterday's trash after we were finished using each other. I explained how though that hurt me, it had become the devil I knew.

I was genuinely surprised to hear myself talk about those things back then. More to the point, I was disappointed in myself, because of this realization: I actually missed being used and discarded. It was all I knew. It was awful, but it was what I had come to expect. Somehow the situation felt "off" because that abusive element wasn't a part of it.

Though I liked the kindness, it unnerved me too. I kept waiting for the other shoe to drop. I wouldn't let myself get too comfortable with him, just in case. It was at that moment that I realized just how truly broken I was, and how truly broken we all were.

We talked about that, too.

In many ways, Danny helped me to embark on the first step towards writing this book. It took me the better part of four years and a lot of personal reflection, magical and mundane work on myself, and a willingness to admit that I was complicit in the things that broke me. If I'm honest, however, the healing started with Danny's insistence on bringing the humanity back into that first encounter all those years ago.

Looking back on it now, it only seems appropriate that the culminating event that helped me recognize my healing would have also involved Danny. We had been trying (unsuccessfully) to get together for six months, but he still lived in Durham and I had moved to Greensboro. Our schedules were opposite each other, and he had to travel out of state quite a bit for work.

When we finally did get together in March, he was hornier than I had ever seen him. Over text, as he was driving to my place, he flat-out told me that he was going to need to "use me something hard" and he wanted to know if I could handle that. I told him that, for him, I could.

I had been studying witchcraft quite a bit more intensely since our last encounter, and I had started to recognize the value of Martial sex. Previously, I had only ever wanted the Venusian variety. Martial sex is the kind that involves just base, animalistic lust, whereas Venusian-style sex is the romantic, gentle, lovemaking that we all know so much about. Anyway, because of my magical studies, I had begun to acknowledge something I never had before: sometimes people just need to regulate their hormones and release the pent-up sexual energies that "clog" their systems. I was in a much better place to handle what he needed in that moment than I had been in years past, and I told him so.

When he got to the house, he was primal. He was more aggressive than I was prepared for. It wasn't bad. Like I said, I had a history with Danny, and I knew I could trust him no matter what happened. It was just unexpected.

He wanted me naked when he arrived, so there were no clothes for him to rip off, except his own. He pushed me against the wall and kissed me. As we made our way to the bedroom like pinballs, he ripped off his garments one by one, leaving them strewn across my floor.

The actual intercourse, itself, was just as aggressive. It lasted for the better part of 40 minutes before he collapsed on top of me, but when he was finished, he pulled me into him and held me close, just like old times.

"Thank you," he whispered into my ear. "I needed that."

I nodded, as I pressed myself against him.

"What can I do for you now?" he asked.

I just got quiet. I legitimately didn't know how to answer him.

Apparently, the silence echoed through the room, though, because he repeated his question.

"I don't know, Danny."

I hated to admit it, but I genuinely didn't know. Sex really hasn't been my strong suit. Of course I've had plenty of sex. Most Gay men have had more than our fair share of sex. I'm no different. In fact, despite my history of sexual dysfunction, I'm actually quite good at the act itself from all the practice, but I've never really enjoyed the experience outside of a relationship.

I have done it on dates, because it was expected, and I wrongly believed that it would lead to future dates with that man. The truth is that sex is never the reason a guy will or won't go out on a second date. If he really likes you, it won't matter either way, and the natural course of your relationship will unfold as it should. If you have sex on the first date, he won't shame you for it. If you don't, he won't write you off. However, it took me a very long time to learn that lesson.

I have had sex in the past as a hookup because I was bored, or I just needed companionship, or I was overwhelmed by my body's sex drive. In all of those cases, though, I always resented both the sex and the other person. I resented the hookup for not wanting a deeper connection beyond the brief arranged encounter, and I resented my body for forcing the issue. Some people find this fact odd, but it is the truth. I have resented my sex drive in the past. I felt that it was just too demanding.

Regardless of whether that's crazy or not (and, honestly, I'm fairly certain it is), the resentment (all the resentments) prevented me from appreciating those previous sexual encounters with men. There was no resentment with Danny, and I was glad to give my body to him in whatever way he needed it in that moment.

Over the years, we had built a sense of respect and trust. It didn't matter that we were only in the same room a handful of times or that our last physical encounter happened three years earlier. We just seemed to click.

"Okay," he said, "Will you trust me to try something else?"

I repositioned myself so that he could see me arch my eyebrow and smirk in his general direction.

He laughed and said, "No seriously. Will you let me try something?"

"What is it?" I asked.

He explained that he wanted to "go deep" and try to push through the "third gate."

I just laughed and said, "Danny, there is no third gate!" I assumed he was talking about the sphincters. Apparently, I was wrong.

Now it was his turn to give me the raised eyebrow. "It's a mystical gate. Why do I have to explain this to a witch?!"

I just chuckled. Clearly, we had run up against an area where my magical training was deficient. I was aware that pushing past the second sphincter could feel drastically different than more "shallow play," but I had never heard of a "third gate"—mystical or otherwise.

"Let me just take care of you for a bit," he said. Then he explained to me how it would work. He wanted to lay me on my back so he could push past the second sphincter. He told me it might feel slightly uncomfortable at first but that if I relaxed, took deep calming breaths, and kept eye contact with him, that would pass. Danny clearly intended to use some hypnosis on me. (Those are the exact things I say to hypnosis clients all the time, albeit without the sexual component.) Ostensibly, it was after that moment that I would begin to "see unicorns, fairy dust, and sparkles."

I laughed again, which made him laugh, which made his golden-brown eyes twinkle.

"Okay, Danny. I'm game, but if I don't see at least one unicorn".

He put his finger up to my mouth to shut me up, and he smiled as he said, "You will. Now just relax."

I'll be honest. I was a bit nervous when it started, but the way Danny looked at me, the way he kept eye contact actually did calm me down. He mouthed the words "I got you" and smiled, which made me smile back. In the beginning, he was slow and gentle. It was so drastically different than the last round that I couldn't help take notice.

As he passed the "second gate," I wanted nothing more than to stop him and call the whole thing off, but he must have sensed it. Maybe my body tensed up. I'm sure it did. I looked away and shut my eyes tight.

He said, "Look at me."

When I did, he smiled and slowed down the pace a little more, though he didn't lose any ground. He never pulled back.

"You are doing so well, babe."

That one bit of praise seemed to be all I needed from him in that moment because, all of a sudden, the discomfort went away, and he was able to move forward easily and effortlessly. Within a matter of moments, he was deeper than any man had ever gone before. I felt like I had been filled up. It was an odd, but strangely arousing feeling.

When he finally got all the way in, he stopped. He smiled at me again and told me how proud of me he was for taking it all. Then he asked, "You ready?"

I nodded.

He lifted my chin and leaned in to kiss me.

Then as if out of nowhere my vision began to fade in and out. I may have actually closed my eyes. I don't know. After the fact, Danny told me that there were several times that my eyes actually rolled back. This moment may have been one of those times.

What I do know is that I actually did see flashes of light before

I lost myself to the sensations. I'm not sure how much time actually elapsed, but when I came back, Danny was there smiling at me. It lasted a brief moment or two longer before we both came in a moment of wild release. For me, it was that smile and the twinkle in his eyes as I felt him fill me up. He told me it was pretty much the same for him. The face I made when I opened my eyes got him there.

Anyway, I learned a valuable lesson that day. Just because sex is happening outside of a committed relationship doesn't mean that it has to be "dirty" or shameful. Two people can enjoy each other's bodies in a way that is still respectful and meaningful in the moment. Whether or not a sexual encounter is healthy, or damaging, is more about how the people involved handle the experience than what the experience itself actually entails.

12 GAY LOVE

Love rules the great mysteries of the witch's faith. As Diane Morrison said in her June 2013 *Patheos* article titled *Seekers and Guides: The Three Degrees of Wicca*, "The Mystery is Love and Sex: how the joining together of two creates something greater than the sum of its parts."[87] Gay men have participated in this mystery since time immemorial. History and myth document that truth.

Plato routinely recognized love between two men as the most noble form of love. James Neill quotes Plato as saying, "homosexual love shared the evil reputation of philosophy and gymnastics in 'countries which are subject to the barbarians,' because '[homosexual relationships] are inimical to tyranny … Our own tyrants learned this lesson through bitter experience, when the love between Aristogeiton and Harmodius grew so strong that it shattered their power. Whenever, therefore, it has been established that it is shameful to be involved in sexual relationships with men, this is due to evil on the part of legislators, to despotism on the part of the rulers, and to cowardice on the part of the governed."[88]

To see that Plato is correct, all one has to do is turn to our own current government. The legislation that is continuously proposed against Gay men and LGBTQIA people in general is truly heinous. Being bitch slapped in the face with that harsh part of Plato's wisdom, I can think of no better remedy for the situation than to implement the awesome strength of the love he also professes. That is what this book is about: helping Gay men reclaim the transcendent love with each other that is our birthright—so much the better if we manage to topple despots in

---

[87] Morrison, Diane. "Seekers and Guides: The Three Degrees of Wicca." *Patheos*, 2013. www.patheos.com/blogs/agora/2013/06/seekers-and-guides-the-three-degrees-of-wicca/

[88] Neill, James. *The Origins and Role of Same-Sex Relations in Human Society*. McFarland & Company Inc., 2009, 169.

the process!

The ancient world prized the loving union of two pair-bonded men above all other unions. Like Diotima said in Plato's *Symposium*, everyone respected the offspring of Gay relationships—virtue, great works of art, refinement of thinking, etc. In fact, as I pointed out earlier, she goes on to say that everyone preferred the offspring of these unions because they produced a level of personal immortality for the two men involved. Though giving birth to children ensured that one's genes would influence future generations, biological reproduction did very little (if anything) to ensure the actual immortality of the parents' personal or divine egos.

A cursory study of history actually seems to back up Diotima's claim about this particular benefit of homosexual relationships. Hoplology [89] recorded the deeds of The 300, and their homosexuality has become part and parcel of their memorial even to this day. It is common knowledge amongst military historians that Alexander the Great adored Hephaiston above all others. Marcel Proust, Ralph Waldo Emerson, and William S. Burroughs are just a few of the modern literary figures who scaled the heights of Olympus and sipped from Ganymede's cup in the footsteps of men like Homer, Hesiod, and Virgil. Michelangelo and Leonardo da Vinci are both artists who benefited in the same way.

The Greeks did an incredible job of mythologizing the awesome power and beauty of our loving relationships with each other. In fact, their artistry was so masterful that, to this day, the modern imagination immediately swings to thoughts of the Greeks whenever the topic of "classical homosexuality" is brought up. Some people claim that the most iconic depiction of Gay love in all of the various world mythologies comes from a Greek epic: the *Iliad*. Byrne R. S. Fone says, "Achilles and Patroclus stand as exemplars of ideal male love, of a fidelity and a loyalty such that both are willing to die for each other; they are invoked as such by most Greek writers, and their passion came to

---

[89] The study of human combat.

be seen as the central and most dramatic element of the story and indeed as the founding text against which all subsequent tales of love between men were measured."⁹⁰

Whether that's true or not, one thing is certain. Achilles' sorrow over the death of Patroclus definitely showed just how powerful the bond between two men can be. In his grief and anger, Achilles turned the tides and toppled an entire city state as he sought vengeance for his lover's death. The *Iliad* makes no bones about the fact that this single event decided the outcome of the Trojan War.

Because of a quarrel with Agamemnon, Achilles refused to fight in the battle to recapture Troy. Fearing that the war would be lost without Achilles' intervention and wanting to fool the Trojans into thinking that Achilles was actually present on the battlefield, Patroclus asked Achilles to borrow his armor. Unfortunately, this is the very act that gets Patroclus killed, and, upon hearing of his comrade's death, Achilles vowed revenge against Hector.

Achilles called upon his mother, the sea goddess Thetis, to aid him in seeking his revenge, and she equipped him with new armor. (Hector claimed his old armor along with Patroclus' body as trophies, but he did not get to enjoy the spoils of war for long.) When Achilles rejoined the war, he decimated the Trojan troops to get to Hector, and when he finally did come face-to-face with the Trojan warrior in battle, his response is so ferocious that it shocked even his own troops.

As an interesting side note, James Neill claims the love between Achilles and Patroclus was influenced by the *Epic of Gilgamesh*. "In succeeding centuries the *Epic of Gilgamesh* became widely disseminated throughout the Middle East. Copies were produced over a period of nearly 2,000 years and have been found in several languages in locations as diverse as the remains of the Hittite capital in what is now Turkey, and in Palestine. The influence of the epic can even be seen in the *Illiad* [sic] and *Odessey* [sic] of

---

⁹⁰ Fone, Byrne R. S. *The Columbia Anthology of Gay Literature*. Columbia University Press, 1998, 17.

Homer."[91] In my opinion, the only reason that Byrne R. S. Fone and others like him are able to make the claim that Achilles and Patroclus are THE iconic version of homosexual love is because Western society has willfully turned a blind eye away from the relationship between Gilgamesh and Enkidu. The loving bond between these two men is so essential to the story that homophobes have repeatedly failed in their attempts to write the homosexuality out. However, it was easier to gloss over the homosexuality of the Greek myths, and so they received more attention.

While Achilles and Patroclus may be the archetypal warrior lovers within Greek myth, they are not the only example for us to turn to in the ancient Hellenic world. Hercules had more male lovers than most of the other gods and men combined. He had intimate relationships with both handsome Hylas and war-like Iolaus, but "we are told he loved wise Nestor best …"[92] By some accounts, his male lovers were legion. However, even the myths of Hercules are not the extent of our resources. There were also instances of the Greek gods prizing one mortal youth above all others for us to turn to for inspiration.

Some say that Zeus lays claim to the honor of having created homosexuality when he was "set on fire" by the sight of Ganymede's thighs. Others say that Poseidon was the first god to love another man when he fell for Pelops, or perhaps Kaineus, to whom he granted invulnerability in exchange for his love.[93] Regardless of which god created homosexuality in that cosmology, the point is that both Gods participated in loving unions with other men. While Poseidon lusted for Pelops and their relationship ultimately ended when Pelops married a woman, Zeus' love for Ganymede was everlasting. He adored the boy so much that he made him immortal and appointed him his

---

[91] Neill, James. *The Origins and Role of Same-Sex Relations in Human Society.* McFarland & Company Inc., 2009, 92.

[92] Calimach, Andrew. *Lovers' Legends The Gay Greek Myths.* Haiduk Press, 2002, 7.

[93] Calimach, Andrew. *Lovers' Legends The Gay Greek Myths.* Haiduk Press, 2002, 4.

cupbearer.

The list of Greek gods who had intimate relationships with other men is so extensive that it would take an entire book dedicated to that one topic alone to do it justice. To preserve space and to move onto other cultures, I have chosen to only highlight long-term and loving pair-bonded or God-mortal relationships between men. Should you wish to investigate this topic further, there will be no shortage of material available to you.

Our love transcended the realm of myth and legend. Both history and literature memorialize male lovers around the world. In China, it is assumed that the West introduced homosexuality into their culture, which as James Neill says, "is especially ironic since China, alone among the world cultures, has an unbroken documented history of homosexuality covering nearly three thousand years, from the early Zhou dynasty until the 20th century."[94]

One of the most famous accounts of homosexuality was recounted by the famous legal philosopher Han Fei Zi in his *Basic Writings*. During the Zhou Dynasty, a young man named Mizi Xia won favor with Duke Ling, the ruler of the feudal state of Wei in the late sixth century B.C.E. According to Han Fei, the state of Wei had a law under which anyone who made use of the ruler's carriage without permission would be punished by having his feet amputated. When the young lover of the Duke found out that his mother had taken ill, he forged an order from the Duke and "borrowed" the carriage to rush to her side. Rather than punish Mizi Xia, the Duke was so moved that he praised his lover for this act of love and devotion in the face of personal peril. On another occasion, the two lovers were walking through the orchard, and Mizi Xia picked a peach and bit into it. He thought it was so delicious that he offered the remaining half to the Duke, who exclaimed, "How sincere is your love for me! You forgot your own appetite and think only of giving me good things to eat!"

Unfortunately, as time went on and Mizi Xia lost the beauty of his youth, the Duke grew tired of him. When one of Mizi Xia's

---

[94] Neill, James. *The Origins and Role of Same-Sex Relations in Human Society*. McFarland & Company Inc., 2009, 234.

rivals at court began to spew venom into the Duke's ear, the Duke began to change his tune about his lover. Now instead of finding honor in risking life and limb to rush to an ailing mother or grace and generosity in sharing a peach, the Duke is reported to have said, "he once stole my carriage, and another time he gave me a half-eaten peach!"[95] The moral of the story here is that everything depends on perspective. The simplest event can be made romantic by one who is in love, and the most noble gesture can be made base by one who has been jaded or embittered. Though the Duke is clearly a cad for abandoning someone just because he aged out of youth, Mizi Xia was at fault too. It is not Mizi Xia's fault that he aged. However, it is certainly his fault that he tested his lover's patience and took so many liberties throughout his youth.

The other archetypal story of homosexuality in Chinese history involves the love of the last Han emperor, Emperor Ai, for Dong Xian. An anonymous historian describes the iconic moment between the two lovers: "Emperor Ai was sleeping in the daytime with Dong Xian stretched out across his sleeve. When the emperor wanted to get up, Dong Xian was still asleep. Because he did not want to disturb him, the emperor cut off his own sleeve and got up. His love and thoughtfulness went this far!"[96]

Emperor Ai loved Dong Xian so much that he named Dong Xian his successor, turning to ancient mythical precedents to do so. Ultimately, this did not go well, because Dong Xian had too many political enemies. Despite the fact that Emperor Ai turned over the imperial seals to Dong Xian, making him emperor, he was forced to commit suicide.

These two singular events (the half-eaten peach and the cut sleeve) became symbols of homosexuality in Chinese culture on par with the Rainbow Flag or the pink triangle before it. During Emperor Ai's lifetime, men in the imperial court took to cutting off one sleeve in honor of the kindness and devotion the emperor

---

[95] Neill, James. *The Origins and Role of Same-Sex Relations in Human Society*. McFarland & Company Inc., 2009, 237.

[96] Neill, James. *The Origins and Role of Same-Sex Relations in Human Society*. McFarland & Company Inc., 2009, 245.

showed toward his lover. This fashion trend ultimately led to the cut sleeve, like the half-eaten peach, being taken more generally as a euphemism for homosexual love and devotion by later generations.[97]

The martial world of Japan's samurai where valor, masculine accomplishment, and the male physique are glorified, was a fertile ground in which to grow intimate and loyal relationships between men. The samurai didn't just take male lovers when more-desirable female partners were scarce. Unlike other warrior societies in other cultures, the samurai preferred their homosexual bonds. "In this masculine society, women were looked down upon, viewed by many of the knights as mere 'holes to be borrowed' for carrying the children of warriors."[98]

Over the centuries of samurai rule, the relationships between samurais and their *wakashu*[99] developed into a rich tradition of "noble love," with its own etiquette, ideals and standards of honor.[100] Unlike the monks of ancient Japan, the samurai did not like young or androgynous-looking boys. Instead, they preferred boys who were in their late teens and early twenties. In stark contrast to the Greeks, who had a similar form of sexual custom, the samurai preferred their wakashu to look like men. "They preferred big, muscular boys, and bore cuts on their bodies as a sign of male love."[101]

Both cultures infused their love for these young men with an idealism which linked romance and valor. Supposedly, the samurai's attraction for his wakashu was due more to the wakashu's virtues—qualities like strength and courage that

---

[97] Neill, James. *The Origins and Role of Same-Sex Relations in Human Society.* McFarland & Company Inc., 2009, 245.

[98] Neill, James. *The Origins and Role of Same-Sex Relations in Human Society.* McFarland & Company Inc., 2009, 278.

[99] The samurai word for their young squires was wakashu, which meant "young man").

[100] Neill, James. *The Origins and Role of Same-Sex Relations in Human Society.* McFarland & Company Inc., 2009, 278-279.

[101] Neill, James. *The Origins and Role of Same-Sex Relations in Human Society.* McFarland & Company Inc., 2009, 279.

inflamed the samurai's passions. In fact, the greatest honor that one of the wakashu could achieve was to give his life in battle to save his master's.

The idealistic romance between a samurai knight and his wakashu was established on the widespread, ancient belief that a man's virtuous qualities and masculine skill would pass into a younger male during intercourse. Once again, we see the remnants of a connection back to the ancient headhunting practices. For the samurai, the gift of the established knight's virtue was not a one-sided venture. Far from it. In fact, the samurai honored the sexual submission of the wakashu. The older lover (the *nenja*) had an obligation to provide the younger man with an education and emotional support, smooth the way for him socially, and above all, maintain his own reputation so as to serve as an appropriate role model during the younger man's apprenticeship. In fact, both men vowed to uphold the manly virtues of the samurai: loyalty, steadfastness, and honor.[102]

These relationships were not just educational. There are countless stories of samurai knights remaining in deeply committed, passionate, loving relationships with each other long after the wakashu's apprenticeship was over. In some cases, these relationships lasted their entire lives. Unlike the Greeks, the age factor was less important (if not entirely irrelevant) to the samurai. Instead, the important factor was the wakashu's willingness to submit himself to the nenja. These pair-bonded warrior relationships existed between men of the same age as well as older and younger men. Samurai culture even allowed the older man to take the role of wakashu in these long-standing relationships without suffering shame or ridicule.

For most Western Gay men today, it would be odd to think of Islam as tolerant of homosexuality. According to the *Al Hadis*, however, a collection of sayings attributed to their Prophet, homosexual love is one of the promised pleasures of Paradise. In fact, throughout the entire history of Islam, there is a robust tradition of same-sex love between men, complete with poetry

---

[102] Neill, James. *The Origins and Role of Same-Sex Relations in Human Society.* McFarland & Company Inc., 2009, 280.

and literature. Even in the face of the modern religious interpretation, this rich cultural heritage of male love has continued to thrive.

During the height of the Ottoman Empire, Islamic influences were added to those of the Greeks, Romans, and Slavs, which produced the diverse ethnic, religious, and cultural character of the Balkans that we see even today.[103] The 20th-century psychologist Havelock Ellis noted that while homosexual relationships were more popular with the Muslim men in the region, even the local Catholic priests gave their official blessing to these unions. While staying in the Balkans, Paul Näcke, a German psychologist and criminologist famous for his writings on homosexuality,[104] said that his innkeeper (a Christian) had formed a blood pact with another man in order to solidify their "masculine love." Näcke wrote that "each pricked the other in the finger and sucked out a drop of blood. Now each has to protect the other till death."[105]

As with Achilles and Patroclus, the lovers of China, and the samurai, we see a recurrent theme develop in these exclusive male relationships within the Muslim world. Regardless of cultural trappings, there seems to be an almost universal acknowledgement of a commitment involving loyalty and devotion between the two men, which supersedes all other ties. Though no one tradition of male love is whole or complete, that does not mean that we must despair. When looked at from a universal perspective, there is enough documentation to begin reclaiming this beautiful component of Gay life. *And we must reclaim it!*

As I have said in countless other places in this book and in *Garbed In Green*, the Gay Community is tearing itself apart because of the rampant disregard and abuses we subject each other to on

---

[103] Neill, James. *The Origins and Role of Same-Sex Relations in Human Society.* McFarland & Company Inc., 2009, 314.

[104] Näcke is the man responsible for coining the term *narcissist* in 1899. Some scholars even credit him with transmuting sex between two men from a simple activity into an identity.

[105] Neill, James. *The Origins and Role of Same-Sex Relations in Human Society.* McFarland & Company Inc., 2009, 315.

a daily basis. It is not those who routinely picket Gay Pride that endanger us, the politicians, nor the Christian Right. The truth is that no enemy can tear us down if we combine the awesome power of our united wills. The biggest threat to our own safety is the way we treat each other—the fact that we use each other to soothe our own egos and then abandon each other, perpetuating the cycle of shame, guilt, and resentment, thus feeding the stereotypes and misconceptions used by our enemies.

However, as we have begun to see, this rampant abuse was not always our way. The Austrian diplomat Johann Georg von Hahn quoted an Albanian Muslim talking about homosexuality in the region in 1854. The Muslim man is reported to have said, "The lover's feeling for [another man] is pure as sunshine. It places the beloved on the same pedestal as a saint. It is the highest and most exalted passion of which the human breast is capable …".[106]

---

[106] Neill, James. *The Origins and Role of Same-Sex Relations in Human Society.* McFarland & Company Inc., 2009, 315.

13 A NEED-FIRE RITE FOR LOVE

We spent a great deal of time up to this point helping you set your intention before we ever tried to bring a lover into your life. There was a reason for that. If you have been following along with the exercises and practices in this book, you should be in an ideal position to cast this spell and achieve magical success. If you haven't been doing the exercises and practices before you reached this point, go back and do them now before attempting to cast the magic detailed here.

There is no point in casting a love spell when all you really want is a sexual release. Conversely, there is no point in daydreaming about a one-night stand becoming a loving partner or lamenting the fact that a friend with benefits doesn't want to make the situation exclusive. By understanding your actual desires, removing the shame factor, and no longer trying to live up to another's expectations, you are in less danger of making mistakes and having your heart broken. If you take the time to look at yourself objectively and be honest about what you really want, there is less chance that you will feel disappointed or bitter after the encounter.

We all mislabel relationships from time to time. We say we want love, but then we jump right into sex before we even get to know each other. Conversely, we say that we are only searching for sex and then, because the guy is hot, good in bed, or we're just tired of being alone, we "get the feels."

Witches have a tool to help us get around this drama. We call it *The Witch's Pyramid*. It helps us to align our Will and gives us a better chance at success—magically and mundanely. This book has been built around that tool.

The four foundational principles of this pyramid are *To Know, To Dare, To Will, and To Keep Silent*. These principles help the witch establish his true intentions and implement them according to his purpose. All of the exercises in this book were designed to get you to know yourself better and to unify your Will. Go back and take a look at the results of those exercises.

When you killed Prince Charming and claimed his power for yourself, did you feel any which way about it? Did you move on or did you dwell upon the loss of the ideal? Were you upset because you felt like romance had died right along with him, or did you have a new sense of hope? Did fear or loneliness creep up on you?

If you aren't able to answer those questions in a positive way, then ask yourself this. Did you actually do the journaling before the ritual? Be honest with yourself. There's no shame in admitting the truth. You haven't upset me or anyone else, and nobody is judging you.

If you didn't do the journaling component of that rite, make the commitment to yourself to go back and redo it before moving on to casting this spell. You'll be glad you did when you're successful and you have the love you want. Take the full two weeks and really assess Prince Charming's hold on you. Then redo the Sacred Claiming ritual and work your way through this book again. Redo all the exercises in your new mental state. I know you're anxious to find love, but take the time to make sure the man you attract is the right one for you. That way, you won't have to go through this again unnecessarily.

If you did all the exercises as they were written and you feel good about them, you still need to go back and review your work. When you go back and review what you have committed to paper, however, you may find odd discrepancies have crept in without your awareness. If so, iron them out now before continuing onto the next step. You may not find anything that needs to be refined. In that case, go on and cast your spells.

For example, let's look at the exercise for prioritizing desires in Chapter 8. When you were prioritizing your desires, did you find yourself wanting a loving, committed relationship but focusing on the physical qualities of your future mate? Did you feel compelled to talk about how muscular or how hung he would be, how young or old he was, or anything similar? Were your thoughts on his sexual desirability? If so, you have not completely aligned your Will. You are talking about finding love but actually focusing on sex. The two events have nothing to do with each other, as hookup culture is so fond of reminding us. When we really love someone, those physical qualities matter less and, in some cases, they cease to matter entirely. It would be better that you focus on issues of compatibility and things that will actually help you share a life together, qualities that will help you love the person more over time.

Once again, there is no shame in confusing the issue here. We all want what we want. However, this discrepancy could be detrimental to your magical success. Why? Because, you run the risk of doing the spell and having nothing happen, or, worse, getting exactly what you think you want and having your heart broken again. Remember, though, it doesn't have to be that way.

You have two choices. Admit that you just want sex. You really don't need a spell to find a willing partner to do that with. Simply download one of the many hookup apps available to you or go to the Gay club. You will find plenty of willing partners. If, however, you either can't be okay with that or you simply want to stick to your guns about aiming for love, then take the qualities that are purely physical off of your list. All of them. Replace them with these two simple statements: "I want a partner who I am sexually attracted to" and "I want a partner that is sexually compatible with me." Then move on.

You know what you find sexually attractive. You don't need to dwell on each individual trait and add unnecessary hurdles in the path of your success. Besides, by focusing exclusively on the exact physical qualities, you eliminate the possibility that someone who is more right for you might come along. For example, I love tall, muscular men. However, I have, from time to time, found myself attracted to muscular men who were shorter than me. I have also been drawn to tall, skinny men who had an ethereal beauty I couldn't quite define. If I had put both *tall* and *muscular* on my list, I would have eliminated the men who were still attractive to me but didn't fit the whole bill. Better just to shoot for mutual sexual attraction and compatibility.

Do the same thing with all the other exercises from this book. Make certain that they establish a clear intention. It doesn't matter what you chose to write down. What does matter is that your Will be completely united towards your goal before attempting this spell. When you are satisfied that you have achieved an iron-clad and unified Will that can propel your success, you are ready to proceed.

Before we get to the actual spell, there are some preparations you will need to make, because they are essential to the spell's success. You will want to make sure that you start your planning for this spell at least two weeks ahead of time. Depending on where you live, you may need more time to secure the necessary location, ingredients and supplies.

Universal Fluid Condenser

On the Sunday night before your spell, take a handful of chamomile. It doesn't matter whether it is fresh or dried. In my best Ina Garten fashion, I will use pre-packaged tea bags if I can't find any other source, and that seems to work just fine. Place the chamomile flowers into a pot and cover them completely with cold water. Cover and boil for approximately 20 minutes. Let the concoction cool with the lid on, then filter the mixture into a clean pot, straining out the chamomile flowers. Though it's less traditional and the quality of the herbs is, admittedly, questionable, using the tea bags makes this part of the process much easier and saves you having to use a second pot. Now, put the concoction back on the stove and reduce it to about 1/4 of a cup. Leave the lid on and let it cool again. Once the extract is fully cooled, add an equal amount of alcohol. I have found vodka works well for this, but denatured alcohol is also appropriate. Add approximately 10 drops of a gold tincture and a drop of your own blood. Store your fluid condenser in a dark purple bottle in a cool, dark place. I recommend keeping it in the fridge, though you don't have to.[107]

Peach Love Elixir

On the designated Friday when you wish to cast your spell, you will need to make your Peach Love Elixir at least 4 hours before beginning your ritual. Buy 7 peaches. Cut 6 of the peaches into slices, removing the pits. Take a bite of the 7th peach and think

---

[107] If you can't afford gold tincture (it can be expensive), you can always look up recipes online.

of the Chinese story as you place it into a 1-quart mason jar. Remember the moral of the story: everything depends on perspective. Commit to seeing the magic in even the most mundane aspects of your life together. Don't fall into the same traps that Mizi Xia or the Duke fell into. Then place the peach slices from the remaining 6 peaches into the jar. Heat water, then pour it over the peaches and let the mixture steep for at least 15 minutes. After the jar is no longer warm to the touch, refrigerate it for 3-4 hours so that the flavors release. Before you get ready to do the spell, strain about 3-6 ounces of the contents of the jar into a clean smaller mason jar, reserving the remaining mixture for your own use in the days following the ritual.

Conjuring Your Lover

On a **Friday** when Venus is well-aspected with a **Full Moon in a fire sign**, wander out to a green meadow, a flourishing garden, or the seashore to perform your spell. Take with you the **cut sleeve**[108] of a comfortable, old shirt, which has your essence on it. This shirt should be the kind that a boyfriend might wear the next morning if he were to unexpectedly stay the night at your place. An **incense** of lignum-aloes, ambergris, or any other sweet-smelling fragrance you enjoy should be reserved for this occasion. Make sure to have enough on hand to get you through at least one week of regularly burning this incense. Burn only this incense in your home for the entire week leading up to the spell. After your lover shows up, you can use this incense to celebrate special occasions within your relationship. You will also want the **universal fluid condenser** described above, as well as the **Peach Love Elixir**. Secure a small- to medium-sized **cauldron** that

---

[108] The sleeve from your old shirt serves the same purpose as Achilles' armor did for Patroclus. It cloaks your partner in your energy and provides him with comfort and protection. I got the idea for this because one of my ex-boyfriend's was always trying to steal my hoodies. At first it was a bit annoying, but, eventually, I got okay with it. I didn't have much of a choice; though it certainly helped that he was cute about it. Whenever I would ask if the shirt he was wearing was mine, he would promptly deny it, saying, "Nope. It's my boyfriend hoodie." Eventually, I stopped asking and just acknowledged the compliment that it was supposed to be.

might be used to cook beans while camping as well as any necessary protective wear and utensils for removing it from the fire after the spell is complete. Other items that will be necessary for this spell are an **almond anointing oil**, any **musical devices** that you need to play your songs, and, of course, **the fire itself**.

Friday, exactly one week before you plan to do the spell, light some incense in your bedroom and pleasure yourself as you conjure up thoughts of your future mate. See him already in your life. Feel the joy that this union brings you. Imagine what a perfect day together might be like. Then take the cut sleeve and collect the blood of the red lion.[109] Place it under your pillow and sleep with it there for 7 days, only removing it when you are ready to begin the spell.

Each night before you go to sleep leading up to the spell, light some of the same incense in an appropriate censor or container and let yourself drift off to sleep with thoughts of your lover filling your mind. The more realistic you can make these thoughts, the better. Actually feel him in the bed next to you, but do not let the perception of a man in your bed arouse you. You must refrain from pleasuring yourself until the night of the spell. Use the River of Rejuvenation Exercise to calm your passions, if you need to.

On the night of the Full Moon, journey to your secluded location and set up your ritual space. For this rite, build a small fire around your cauldron and have it lit before the ritual so that you save time.

(1) Begin by lighting a self-igniting charcoal disk about 5-10 minutes before you wish to start the ritual. Then, when you are ready to begin, anoint yourself with the almond oil on your forehead. You may use any method of this that calls to you, but

---

[109] As I said, in *Garbed In Green*, blood of the red lion is a witchy euphemism for semen. This reminds me. Only use the smallest amount of semen possible. I know two Gala witches who frequently raise energy by having sex with each other. The first time they attempted one of our rites, they drenched their pearl towelette in both of their fluids, which was hot for them until they realized the damn thing wouldn't burn. You have to make sure that the pearl towelette (or, in this case, the cut sleeve) is dry enough to catch fire. Better to use a little than ruin the spell by not being able to complete the instructions. Truth be told, blood of the red lion is so potent that even the smallest amount is enough to do the job. Ask any woman who ever heard, "Just the tip."

an easy method is to simply draw an Earth Invoking Pentagram on your forehead and say something like, **"May I have the sight to see him."** Then draw another Earth Invoking Pentagram on your chest and say, **"May my heart be open to him."** Finally, draw a third Earth Invoking Pentagram over your phallus and say, **"May our bodies bring each other pleasure."** Now throw some of your designated love incense onto the coal and carry the fire safe vessel around the ritual space in a widdershins direction. Gently fan the smoke and allow it to waft through the air as you move. Focus your thoughts on attracting your love into your life. If you so desire, you can use any words or actions that call to you above and beyond this. You can use a famous love poem that has always spoken to you, a prayer or hymn that calls to you, or something creative that you write special for just this occasion. However, just continuing your nightly visualizations, which you have practiced over the last week, should be enough if nothing else calls to you. What's important is that the entire atmosphere of this rite be enjoyable to you. Make it pleasant.

(2) Dance lightly widdershins in a circular direction to get the energy moving around your space. Pick a song that is slow to medium in tempo, something you can lose yourself in but not something that will exhaust you as you dance.

(3) Invoke the aid of the Gay lovers of myth:

> "I CALL, great Love, the source of sweet delight,
> Holy and pure, and charming to the sight;
> Darting, and wing'd, impetuous fierce desire,
> With Gods and mortals playing, wand'ring fire:
> Agile and twofold, keeper of the keys
> Of heav'n and earth, the air, and spreading seas;
> Of all that Ceres' fertile realms contains,
> By which th' all parent Goddess life sustains,
> Or dismal Tartarus is doom'd to keep,
> Widely extended, or the sounding deep;
> For thee all Nature's various realms obey,

> Who rul'st alone, with universal sway.
> Come, blessed pow'r, regard these mystic fires,
> And far avert unlawful mad desires."[110]

(4) Toss the cut sleeve with the blood of the red lion into the fire and confidently say, **"Favors of the cut sleeve are generous."**

(5) Then take the fluid condenser and administer 10 drops into the mason jar of Peach Love Elixir, focusing on your desire to bring your lover to you. Say: **"In love, I come to thee."** Swirl the jar to mix the liquids, and as you do so impregnate the Elixir with your wish to find a compatible, loving partner.

(6) Carefully pour the contents of the mason jar into the cauldron and say, **"Love of the half-eaten peach never dies."** Allow the liquid, which is loaded with your wish, to evaporate. While the water is evaporating, direct your attention to the rising steam and concentrate on the idea that the wish is absorbed by the Air element and that the most subtle Air principle is aiding you in realizing your wish. Persist with this focused concentration until the last drop of the liquid evaporates. Remove the cauldron from the fire, using the appropriate protections and instruments, keeping best fire safety practices in mind.

(7) Then end this Need-Fire Rite with another round of dancing. The song can be the same song or something with a similar tempo, but this time dance deosil with the intention of closing the energy down. As I said, in *Garbed In Green*, if you invoked something, you must release it. If you opened something, you must close it. You don't have to worry about releasing Love. Its energies are ever-present, but if you modified this rite in any way, just be mindful of this axiom.

(8) Include a feast of delicious foods that bring you pleasure and enjoy yourself until the fire goes out. Have fun with yourself

---

[110] In *Garbed In Green* I appealed to *The Orphic Hymns* for the invocations, and I saw no reason not to do so again in this spell. Within *The Orphic Hymns* is a hymn to Love, which seemed appropriate for use here because it calls on Love as an energy, not a Goddess. For Gay men, I thought that was important, which is why I repeated the practice. This is hymn LVIII within *Orphic Hymns*.

and just get lost in the loving energies which you have conjured forth.

Should you not be able to perform this spell outside, you can modify it as you see fit to work with your current living situation. Instead of a bonfire, you might use a portable gas stove that is safe for indoor use. Make sure to follow all of the directions that come with it and adhere to normal fire safety practices. If you choose to use the portable gas stove, you might also consider replacing the cauldron with a metal bowl or a regular cooking pot. Modify these instructions to fit your own purposes.

BIBLIOGRAPHY

Aristotle. *Nicomachean Ethics*. Translated by Roger Crisp, Cambridge University Press, 2000.

Atkinson, W. W. and Edward E. Beals. *Desire Power or Your Energizing Forces*. Robert Collier Book Corp, 1975.

_____. *Regenerative Power or Vital Rejuvenation*. Robert Collier Book Corp, 1975.

Bettelheim, Bruno. *The Uses of Enchantment: The Meaning and Importance of Fairy Tales*. Alfred A. Knopf Publishing: New York, 1976.

Blavatsky, H. P. *The Secret Doctrine I*. The Theosophical Publishing Company, Limited, *1888*.

Bolotin, David. *Plato's Dialogue on Friendship: An Interpretation of the Lysis, with a New Translation*. Cornell University Press, 1979.

Brown, Mary Ellen, and Bruce A. Rosenbery, editors. *Encyclopedia of Folklore and Literature*. ABC-CLIO, LLC: Santa Barbara, California, 2009.

Calimach, Andrew. *Lovers' Legends The Gay Greek Myths*. Haiduk Press, 2002

Cashorali, Peter. *Fairy Tales: Traditional Stories Retold for Gay Men*. HarperSanFrancisco, 1997.

Cobb, William S. *Plato's Erotic Dialogues*. State University of New York Press, 1993.

Cox, Marian Roalfe. *Cinderella Three Hundred and Forty-five Variants*. Publications of the Folk-Lore Society: London, 1893.

Deslippe, Philip., eds. *The Kybalion The Definitive Edition William Walker Atkinson Writing As Three Initiates*. Jeremy P. Tarcher/Penguin, 2008.

Evans, Arthur. *Witchcraft and the Gay Counterculture*. Fag Rag Books,

1978.

Fone, Byrne R. S. *The Columbia Anthology of Gay Literature.* Columbia University Press, 1998.

Frost, Gavin & Yvonne. *The Witch's Magical Handbook.* Reward Books, 2000.

Giovinco, Casey. *Garbed In Green: Gay Witchcraft and the Male Mysteries.* Publisher: Casey Giovinco, 2018.

Hesiod, Theogony. Translated by Richard S. Caldwell, Focus Publishing, 1987.

Higgins, Patrick, eds. A Queer Reader. The New York Press, 1993.

Illes, Judika. *Encyclopedia of Spirits: the ultimate guide to the magic of fairies, genies, demons, ghosts, gods & goddesses.* Harper One, 2009.

Leitch, Aaron. *Secrets of the Magickal Grimoires: The Classical Texts of Magick Deciphered.* Llewellyn Publications, 2013.

Maas, Vera Sonja. *The Cinderella Test: Would You Really Want The Shoe To Fit?.* ABC-CLIO, LLC, 2009.

Mitchell, Stephen. *Gilgamesh.* Atria Paperback, 2004

Morrison, Diane. "Seekers and Guides: The Three Degrees of Wicca." *Patheos,* 2013. www.patheos.com/blogs/agora/2013/06/seekers-and-guides-the-three-degrees-of-wicca/

Neill, James. *The Origins and Role of Same-Sex Relations in Human Society.* McFarland & Company Inc., 2009.

Ott, Joanne Sienko. *The Crone Archetype: Women Reclaim Their Authentic Self By Resonating with Crone Imagery.* MA Thesis. SOPHIA, 2011. https://sophia.stkate.edu/ma_hhs/17/.

Penczak, Christopher. *Gay Witchcraft: Empowering the Tribe.* Red Wheel/Weiser, LLC, 2003.

Penner, Terry and Christopher Rowe. *Plato's Lysis.* Cambridge University Press, 2005.

Sinnett, A. P. *The Occult World.* Trübner & Co., 1889.

Tyson, Donald, eds. *Three Books of Occult Philosophy written by Henry Cornelius Agrippa of Nettesheim.* Translated by James Freake. Llewellyn Publications, 2013.

Tzu, Han Fei. *Basic Writings.* Translated by Burton Watson, Columbia University Press, 1964.

Willson, William Griffith. *Alcoholics Anonymous: The Story of How Many Thousands of Men and Women Have Recovered from Alcoholism.* Alcoholics Anonymous World Services, Inc., 2001.

Wong, Eva. *Seven Taoist Masters A Folk Novel of China.* Shambhala Classics, 1990.

GETTING IN TOUCH

I would love to hear back from you about your experiences with this book and its rituals. I believe that rediscovery the Male Mysteries must be a collective effort, and I'm excited to participate in that effort with each of you. If you would like to talk with me directly, you can reach me through my website at either:

www.caseygiovinco.com
www.facebook.com/hexebeast/

If you are interested in exploring the Male Mysteries with other Gay and Bisexual Pagan Men, you can join one of the many Facebook groups that Gala Witchcraft maintains as a community service to the general Pagan Public at:

https://www.facebook.com/groups/gaymalewitches/

We also maintain a group for Straight, Bisexual, Gay, as well as Transgender Men at:

https://www.facebook.com/groups/malepaganmysteries/

And, finally, we maintain a group on the Male Mysteries open to anyone who's interested (male, female, Transgender, gay, straight, bisexual, asexual). If you're interested in talking about this book, the book *Garbed In Green*, or the Male Mysteries, in general, it's a great group with a very diverse group of members. You can get in touch there at:

https://www.facebook.com/groups/wiccagarbedingreen/

Finally, if you loved what you read here and you would like to join one of the covens within Gala Witchcraft, you can reach out to us at one of the links below:

A Dangerous Wisdom

www.galawitchcraft.com
https://www.facebook.com/groups/covenmellona/

Thank you again for reading this book. I look forward to meeting you.

Blessed Be,
Casey Giovinco.

ABOUT THE AUTHOR

Casey Giovinco is the Chief Elder of Gala Witchcraft, which combines traditional coven-based, Initiatory Wicca with the central goal of reawakening the Gay Mysteries. Casey works with Gay men as a philosophical consultant and life coach, helping them apply sound occult principles to finding the love they desire. By combining the skills that he developed as an academic philosopher with the wisdom of the Western Mystery Traditions, Casey provides a unique approach to problem solving that helps Gay men to achieve lasting success in their lives.

www.ingramcontent.com/pod-product-compliance
Lightning Source LLC
Chambersburg PA
CBHW071507040426
42444CB00008B/1535